P9-BZZ-647

THE CIRCLE TIME BOOK

for holidays and special occurrences throughout the year

Dedicated to all the young children and adults
who enjoy celebrating holidays throughout the year.
Have fun as you learn and laugh together.

THE
CIRCLE TIME
BOOK

by
Liz & Dick Wilmes

art

Donna Dane

A BUILDING BLOCKS Publication
314 LIBERTY STREET · BOX 31 · DUNDEE · ILLINOIS · 60118

© 1982 by Liz and Dick Wilmes

ISBN 0-943452-00-7
Library of Congress Catalog Card No. 82-072304

Published by BUILDING BLOCKS, 314 Liberty Street—P.O. Box 31,
Dundee, Illinois 60118. All rights reserved. No part of this
publication may be reproduced, stored in a retrieval system, or
transmitted, in any form or by any means, electronic, mechanical,
photocopying or otherwise, without the prior written permission of
the publisher. Printed in the United States of America.

Graphic Consultant: Jeane Everest

Distributed by:
GRYPHON HOUSE, Inc.
P.O. Box 275
Mt. Rainier, MD 20712

ISBN 0-943452-00-7

Holidays are special days and times set aside by people who choose to celebrate them. Some holidays are celebrated for religious, patriotic, and ethnic reasons. Others are celebrated because of the time of year or to honor a certain person. All people do not celebrate all holidays. Many holidays are celebrated differently depending upon personal choice, family custom, ethnic heritage, part of the country, religious background, and so on.

The collection of special events included in THE CIRCLE TIME BOOK introduces young children to a variety of holidays, festivals, and special occurrences. The reader must remember that these holidays are only a beginning. Be sure to enjoy all of the special days that occur for your young children and families throughout the year.

Contents

INTRODUCTION

Circle Time is that segment of the day when the group of young children is gathered together to enjoy participating in a variety of activities. These activities are usually centered around a theme or specific holiday which is also being highlighted during free play, art, lunch, outdoors, and other times of the day. Thus, through a coordinated curriculum, the theme is continually reinforced in many different ways throughout the day.

The ideas in THE CIRCLE TIME BOOK are divided into eight major categories.

For Openers—Each holiday begins with an introductory activity which immediately involves the children in the spirit of that occasion.

Fingerplays—Children enjoy active rhymes. Whenever possible add action to the fingerplays, rhymes, and poems suggested for each holiday.

Recipes—Food is often associated with holidays. Enjoy making special foods with a small group of children at the beginning of the day. Later in the day enjoy eating them with the entire group.

Classroom Visitor—People celebrate holidays in different ways. Classroom visitors should be invited to share the meaning of specific holidays with the children.

Field Trips—Many of the field trips suggested in THE CIRCLE TIME BOOK are within walking distance of most Centers. These trips show the children how the neighborhood is involved with the holiday.

Language Games—The language games expand each child's knowledge of the holiday and enhance the wide range of language, cognitive, small muscle, and social skills. Some of the activities have EXTENSIONS. These are coordinated activities to give your children more experience with a specific concept. Other activities have VARIATIONS. These activities are simply different ways to enjoy the same game. To take full advantage of the language games, the authors suggest that:

- You consider the developmental age of the children, whenever an activity suggests making a "list". If they are not ready for letters, then draw the list using simple pictures.

- Each child has a defined space in which to sit. A small carpet square or a symbol of the holiday (such as a pumpkin taped to the floor at Halloween time) is appropriate.

- The children be exposed to as many "real" objects and examples as possible, such as real food, toys, clothes, flowers, and so on. Models and pictures are necessary, but the more experience children have with the "real", the better understanding they will have of the abstract.

- As many teaching aids, such as felt board pieces, puppets, and objects be available for further exploration during free play times.

Active Games—The active games allow the children to become physically involved with the celebration. At the same time, these games strengthen the child's wide range of physical skills such as balance, coordination, movement, and rhythm.

Books—The suggested books offer only a beginning. Visit your library and choose books you like and will enjoy reading to your group of children.

SCHOOL BEGINS

FOR OPENERS

HAVE ALL OF THE CHILDREN GATHER TOGETHER. BEFORE CALLING EACH CHILD'S NAME SAY THIS VERSE:

GIVE A SMILE, GIVE A CHEER,
LET US KNOW THAT YOU ARE HERE.

THEN CALL A CHILD'S NAME. WHEN THAT CHILD STANDS UP, HAVE THE REST OF THE CHILDREN GIVE A BIG SMILE AND CLAP THEIR HANDS. REPEAT FOR EACH CHILD IN THE GROUP.

FINGERPLAYS

I AM HERE!

TWO LITTLE HANDS

Two little hands go clap, clap, clap.
Two little feet go tap, tap, tap.
One little body turns round and round,
And sits quietly down.

FRIENDS

I say "Hello" to friends at school.
I'm happy as can be.
They are my special school friends.
I like them all, you see.

GOOD DAY EVERYBODY

Good day everybody,
Good day everybody,
Good day! Good day! Good day!

Smile everybody,
Smile everybody,
And chase those blues away.

Shake hands everybody,
Shake hands everybody,
Let's make new friends today.

LITTLE FRIENDS

Two little friends are better than one,
And three are better than two,
And four are much better still.
Just think!
What four little friends can do.

SEPTEMBER

11

● Help the children feel comfortable in the new environment. Take them for a walk around the inside of the school. Go down the hall and visit other classrooms. Show them the washrooms, drinking fountains, fire extinguishers, office, and other places and things of which the children should be aware.

● At another time, take a walk around the outside play yard. Stop at each piece of equipment, talk about how to use the environment and the safety rules. Show the children where the outside riding toys, balls, etc. are kept and how they are stored.

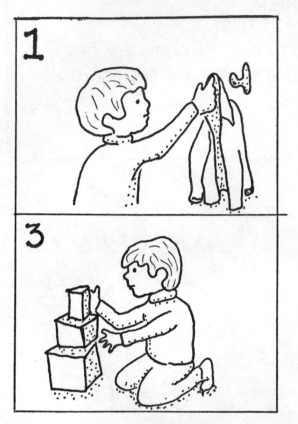

LANGUAGE GAMES

DAILY ROUTINE   A sense of knowing what is going to happen each day will make the children feel more comfortable and help them to adapt to the newness of the experience. Make a chart on a large sheet of poster board showing the progression of activities throughout the day. Talk with the children about the daily routine. After circle time hang the chart low enough on the wall so that all of the children can look at it with ease.

THE CENTERS   Throughout the week, take the group of children to each area of the room. Introduce them to the materials they can use. Discuss how to care for any materials that need special handling, such as covering the playdough and stirring the paint.

END OF THE DAY   Chant *"Children, children, what do you say,*
Which was your favorite thing today?"
Then let each child have an opportunity to say what s/he enjoyed most that day.

ACTIVE GAMES

MOVING

Sing this song to the tune of "*HERE WE GO 'ROUND THE MULBERRY BUSH*". Move around the circle as the group sings.

This is the way we walk to school,
Walk to school, walk to school.
This is the way we walk to school
All on a September morning.

This is the way we glide to school . . .   hop

This is the way we gallop to school . . .

Add other verses with the children.

FEELINGS

Enjoy singing "*IF YOU'RE HAPPY AND YOU KNOW IT, CLAP YOUR HANDS*".

If you're happy and you know it, clap your hands.
If you're happy and you know it, clap your hands.
If you're happy and you know it,
Then your face will really show it.
If you're happy and you know it, clap your hands.

If you're sad and you know it, wipe your eyes.
If you're sad and you know it, wipe your eyes.
If you're sad and you know it,
Then your face will really show it.
If you're sad and you know it, wipe your eyes.

Add other verses as you sing.

BOOKS

SEPTEMBER

HARLOW ROCKWELL — *MY NURSERY SCHOOL*
PETRONELLA BREINBURG — *SHAWN GOES TO SCHOOL*

LABOR DAY

FOR OPENERS

LABOR DAY HONORS ALL WORKERS. BEFORE THE HOLIDAY, MAKE A LIST OF THE PARENTS' OCCUPATIONS IN YOUR GROUP. FIND PICTURES OF AS MANY OCCUPATIONS AS YOU CAN. AS THE CHILDREN ARE COMING TO THE CIRCLE, HOLD UP ONE PICTURE AT A TIME, ASK THE CHILDREN WHAT THE WORKER IS DOING. TALK ABOUT THE OCCUPATIONS. ASK THE CHILDREN IF ANY OF THEIR MOMS OR DADS WORK AT THESE JOBS. IF THEY DO NOT RECOGNIZE THEIR PARENT'S OCCUPATION, SAY "MATTHEW'S MOTHER DRIVES A TAXI. SUE, YOUR FATHER WORKS AT THE GROCERY STORE. DOES HE WORK WITH FOOD?"

ONCE YOU HAVE DISCUSSED ALL OF THE OCCUPATIONS, PLAY A MEMORY GAME. START BY SAYING, "LET'S SEE HOW MANY OF THE JOBS WE CAN REMEMBER." HAVE THE CHILDREN TELL AS MANY OF THEM AS THEY CAN REMEMBER. WHEN THEY BEGIN TO HAVE DIFFICULTY, GIVE THEM CLUES, SUCH AS, "MATTHEW'S MOTHER DRIVES SOMETHING. WHO CAN REMEMBER WHAT IT IS?"

FINGERPLAYS

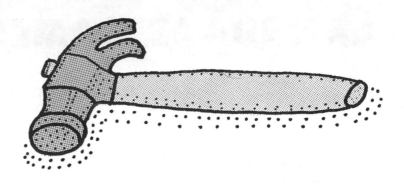

JOHNNY'S HAMMER

Johnny pounds with one hammer,
One hammer, one hammer.
Johnny pounds with one hammer,
All day long.

Johnny pounds with two hammers,
Two hammers, two hammers.
Johnny pounds with two hammers,
All day long.

Johnny pounds with three hammers,

Johnny pounds with four hammers,

Johnny pounds with five hammers,

Johnny now is so tired,
So tired, so tired.
Johnny now is so tired,
All day long.

Johnny goes to sleep now,
Sleep now, sleep now.
Johnny goes to sleep now,
All night long.

THE COBBLER

Crooked heels and scuffy toes
Are all the kinds of shoes he knows.
He patches up the broken places,
Sews the seams and shines their faces.

WHEELS ON THE BUS

The wheels on the bus go round and round,
Round and round, round and round.
The wheels on the bus go round and round,
All through the town.

The people on the bus go up and down,
Up and down, up and down.
The people on the bus go up and down,
All through the town.

The money on the bus goes clink, clank, clunk,

The driver on the bus says, "Move on back,"

The children on the bus say, "Yak, yak, yak,"

The mothers on the bus say, "Sh, sh, sh,"

The wipers on the bus go swish, swish, swish,

The horn on the bus goes honk, honk, honk,

The wheels on the bus go round and round,
Round and round, round and round.
The wheels on the bus go round and round,
All through the town.

SEPTEMBER

15

LANGUAGE GAMES

TALK ABOUT Discuss what the children's moms and dads wear to work. Why do they wear certain types of clothes? Have different uniforms for the children to see. Maybe they can guess from the uniforms what some of the different jobs are that people have. Are some of the clothes specially designed for safety?

TOOLS Before circle time, gather as many tools as you can that represent the occupations of the parents — hammer, wheel, typewriter, chalk, mailbag, shovel, etc. Let the children identify the tool and then tell in what occupation that tool is used. After circle time, put the safe tools on the Discovery Table so that the children have an opportunity to explore them.

CREATIVE THINKING Ask the children *"What job would you like to do when you grow up?"* Some of the children might have reasons why they want to do a certain thing. Give them the opportunity to express their reasons.

ACTIVE GAMES

DO AS I DO Play the game using the occupations of the children's parents. Pretend that you are working at an occupation, such as a carpenter. The children do the same. As everyone is pretending to do a specific job, chant several times, *"I'm a carpenter, hammering and sawing."* Switch to another occupation, such as a typist. Chant while pretending to type, *"I'm a typist, typing, typing, typing, typing."* Continue the game using other familiar occupations.

BOOKS

RICHARD SCARRY — *WHAT DO PEOPLE DO ALL DAY?*
TANA HOBAN — *DIG, DRILL, DUMP, FILL*
FRANCOISE — *WHAT DO YOU WANT TO BE?*

GRANDPARENT'S DAY

FOR OPENERS

HAVE A LONG SHEET OF BUTCHER PAPER TACKED TO THE WALL. AFTER SEVERAL CHILDREN HAVE ARRIVED AT THE CIRCLE, SAY "TELL ME ABOUT YOUR GRANDMOTHER AND/OR GRANDAD." MAKE A LIST OF WHAT THEY SAY ON THE PAPER. AS MORE CHILDREN ARRIVE AT THE CIRCLE, THEY CAN TELL ABOUT THEIR GRANDMOTHERS AND GRANDFATHERS. ENCOURAGE THOSE CHILDREN WHO DO NOT HAVE GRANDPARENTS TO TELL ABOUT OLDER PEOPLE THEY KNOW. DUPLICATE THE LIST AND SEND IT HOME TO THE PARENTS.

FINGERPLAYS

GRANDMOTHER, GRANDFATHER

Grandmother, Grandfather, do come in.
Grandmother, Grandfather, how have you been?
Thanks for coming to visit awhile.
We can play some games, we can share a smile.

Grandmother, Granfather, as you leave today,
We're happy you came, glad you could stay.
Your visit has brought us a lot of joy.
Grandparents are special to each girl and boy.

Dick Wilmes

SEPTEMBER

17

CLASSROOM VISITOR

Ask several grandparents to volunteer in the class for an hour or so during the week. While they are there, ask them to join circle time and share stories with the children. They can tell about when they were children. It would be interesting for them to relate some of the games they enjoyed playing. See if any of the games are the same or similar to the ones that children play now.

LANGUAGE GAMES

TALK ABOUT   Have pictures of older people. Give one to each child. Go around the circle, allowing each child a chance to stand and hold up the picture s/he has. The other children can look at the picture and tell what the person is doing, wearing, talking about, and so on. Children may need help forming and expressing their thoughts. Encourage language by asking questions like, *"The grandad looks like he is walking someplace. Where could he be going?"*

CREATIVE THINKING   *"Susie's* (name of child in your group) *grandparents have a problem. Susie is visiting them for the day. They are trying to decide where to take Susie when she wakes up from her afternoon nap. Let's help them. Where do you enjoy going with your grandparents or older friends?"* Let the children answer. Have pictures of different places to stimulate the children's thinking.(A park, ice cream shop, zoo, etc.)

SINGING   To the tune of *"ROW, ROW, ROW YOUR BOAT."*
Thank you, thank you, thank you Grandma (Grandad)
For joining us today.
Thank you, thank you, thanks so much
Hope you have a nice day!

BOOKS

JEANETTE CAINES — *WINDOW WISHING*
MARGOT APPLE — *WHILE THE MOON SHINES BRIGHTLY*
HELEN BUCKLEY — *GRANDMOTHER AND I*
HELEN BUCKLEY — *GRANDFATHER AND I*
BARBARA WILLIAMS — *KEVIN'S GRANDMA*
JANINA DOMANSKA — *THE TURNIP*

MEXICAN INDEPENDENCE DAY

FOR OPENERS

THIS FUN-FILLED HOLIDAY CELEBRATES MEXICO'S INDEPENDENCE FROM SPAIN IN 1821. IT IS OBSERVED OVER A TWO DAY PERIOD WITH FIREWORKS DISPLAYS THROUGHOUT MEXICO ON THE EVENING OF SEPTEMBER 15TH.

HAVE THE CHILDREN WEAR SMOCKS TO CIRCLE TIME. HAVE A LONG PIECE OF BUTCHER PAPER, DIFFERENT COLORS OF TEMPERA PAINT IN SHALLOW DISHES, AND VARIOUS SIZES OF BRUSHES. HAVE THE CHILDREN SIT AROUND THE BUTCHER PAPER. TALK ABOUT ALL THE COLORS IN THE FIREWORKS. AFTER THE DISCUSSION, LET THE CHILDREN PUT A LITTLE PAINT ON THEIR BRUSH AND THEN 'FLICK' THE BRUSH SO THAT THE PAINT SPATTERS ONTO THE PAPER. CONTINUE UNTIL THE 'SKY IS FILLED WITH BRIGHTLY COLORED FIREWORKS'. LET DRY AND HANG UP FOR ALL TO ENJOY.

VIVA MEXICO!

CLASSROOM VISITOR

Have a person who has lived in Mexico visit the class. Ask him/her to bring some of the typical Mexican dress to show the children. Maybe the classroom visitor will talk about Mexican traditions and family life. What games do the children play in Mexico?

SEPTEMBER

SPEAKING   Celebrate Mexican independence by learning how to say:
SPANISH   *"Viva Mexico!"* - Long live Mexico.
                    "Viva la Independencia!" - Long live independence.

PINATAS   Bring a Pinata to circle time. Pinatas can be made in a variety of shapes, such as animals, birds, dolls, and so on. They are filled with edible and non-edible goodies for the children. Let the children tell what kind of treats they would like to put into the pinata. After circle time, put the pinata on the Discovery Table for the children to examine. Maybe in several days the group could break it open.

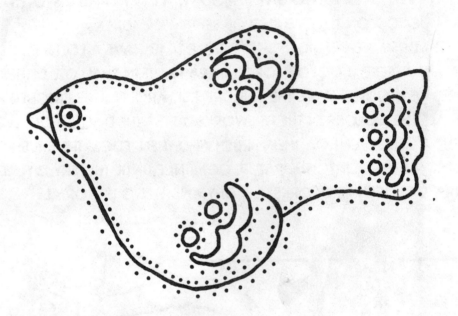

ACTIVE GAMES

PARADES   Mexican Independence is celebrated on September 16th with parades. Make brightly colored vests out of large paper bags during the morning art. In the afternoon, let the children wear the vests and have a parade through the neighborhood.

DANCING   Play Mexican music and let the children dance to the rhythm. If they are not familiar with the music, let them listen first. Begin by clapping to the rhythm and then dancing.

BOOKS

JEAN DE BRUNHOFF — *BABAR TAKES SPANISH LESSONS*

first day of FALL

FOR OPENERS

Art Activity FALL IS A TIME OF BRIGHTLY COLORED LEAVES AND WHIRLING WINDS. MAKE A HANDPRINT TREE WITH THE CHILDREN. GET A LONG SHEET OF BUTCHER PAPER AND PIE PANS FILLED WITH APPROPRIATELY COLORED TEMPERA PAINT. HAVE THE CHILDREN WEAR SMOCKS TO THE CIRCLE. AS THEY ARE GATHERING, BEGIN TO DRAW THE TRUNK OF THE TREE. WHILE DRAWING THE TRUNK, TALK WITH THE CHILDREN ABOUT THE COLORS OF LEAVES AND HOW THEY CHANGE DURING THE FALL SEASON. WHEN ALL OF THE CHILDREN HAVE GATHERED, BEGIN MAKING THE LEAVES OF THE TREE. HAVE CHILDREN DIP THE FLAT OF THEIR HAND INTO THE PAINT AND THEN PRINT IT ONTO THE PAPER. CONTINUE TALKING ABOUT LEAVES AND COLORS UNTIL THE TREE IS FILLED WITH COLORED 'LEAVES'. LET THE CHILDREN WASH THEIR HANDS WHILE THE TREE IS DRYING. WHEN THE TREE IS DRY, HANG IT UP FOR EVERYONE TO ENJOY.

FINGERPLAYS

GRAY SQUIRREL

Gray squirrel, gray squirrel,
Swish your bushy tail.
Gray squirrel, gray squirrel,
Swish your bushy tail.
Wrinkle up your little nose.
Hold a nut between your toes.
Gray squirrel, gray squirrel,
Swish your bushy tail.

GENTLY FALLING LEAVES

Little leaves fall gently down,
Red and yellow, orange and brown.
Whirling, whirling round and round,
Quietly without a sound.

FALL IS HERE

These are the colored leaves
Fluttering down,
And this is the tall tree
Bare and brown.

This is the squirrel
With eyes so bright
Hunting for nuts
With all his might.

This is the hole
Where day by day
Nut after nut
He stores away.

When the winter comes
With its cold and storm,
He'll sleep curled up
All snug and warm.

21

FIELD TRIPS

✳ ● Take a walk. Observe the signs and sounds of Fall. When the group gets back to the room, begin a Seasonal Chart. Get a sheet of butcher paper and list all of the signs and sounds that the children noticed while they were on their walk. After using the chart to talk about the Fall season, put it away so that you will be able to add additional information for the other three seasons.

✳ ● Take another walk. Give each child a bag. While walking, let the children collect colored leaves. During the next free play time, help each child iron his/her leaves between pieces of wax paper. Hang the leaves in a sunny window for all of the children to enjoy.

LANGUAGE GAMES

TALK ABOUT
- The signs of Fall
- Games with leaves
- How animals prepare for winter
- How people prepare for winter

EXPLORING LEAVES
Before exploring the leaves, gather several of each type from the surrounding area. Get a shoe box for each type of leaf and tape a sample onto the side of the box. During the circle time, put the shoeboxes and the other leaves in front of you. Hold up one of the leaves. Have the children look at it. Ask a child to find the box that the leaf belongs in. Hold up another leaf. Then have a different child put it into the correct box. Continue until all of the leaves are sorted.
EXTENSION:
Put the boxes on the Discovery Table for the children to explore during free play time.

EXPLORING SEEDS AND PINECONES
Encourage the children to bring in seeds and pinecones that they find as they are playing outside. Have a special container for each type. When a child brings in a seed or pinecone, pass it around. Have the children touch it, smell it, and then talk about it. Then decide if it is the same as or different than the others. Find the container with the seeds or pinecones that match it or put it in a new container if it is different.

LANGUAGE GAMES

X FELT FUN BOARD

- Make a variety of colored leaves. Put them on the felt board. Talk about all of the colors. Have the children cover their eyes while you take one leaf away. Have them uncover their eyes and tell which leaf is missing.

- Put all of the leaves in a row. Count them. Then say, *"Terry, point to the first leaf."* Continue until you have talked about all of the leaves.

EXTENSION:

Mix up the ordinal words. *"Eric, point to the fifth leaf."* or *"Mary, what color is the third leaf?"*

X LISTEN AND THINK

Say silly things about Fall. Have the children listen carefully and then tell what is incorrect about your statements. For example, *"Listen carefully, I'm going to try to fool you about Fall. Tell me what is wrong with what I say. Ready?"*

"In the Fall the flowers begin to bloom and the grass turns green."

"Birds build their nests in the Fall."

"I love to go sledding and ice skating in the Fall."

SEPTEMBER

ACTIVE GAMES

CREATIVE MOVEMENT

Be leaves in the Fall. *"During the summer you were green and hung tightly to your branch.* (Have the children grasp a pretend branch.) *It is Fall and you are turning beautiful colors. However, the wind is getting stronger* (The teacher should be the wind and begin to blow at the leaves) *and you are twisting on the branch.* (Let the children begin to gently twist.) *The wind gets stronger* (The teacher blows harder) *and you just cannot hang on any longer. You begin to gently fall to the ground.* (Have the children wiggle their bodies slowly, gracefully to the ground.) *You are almost on the ground when a big gust of wind comes along and you pop back up in the air, whirling and twirling for several minutes.* (Have children swoop up and whirl and twirl.) *But the wind settles down and you coast back to the ground.* (Children lying on the ground.) *Here comes the Mom and Dad raking up the leaves.* (The teacher rakes up the leaves. As the leaves are being raked up, have the children roll into the middle of the circle and lie quietly.) *Along comes a gentle breeze and the leaves roll out of the pile."* (Have the children sit up.)

EXTENSION:

Ask the *"leaves"* what might have happened while they were in the pile. Play again and add different endings.

BOOKS

ROBERT McCLOSKY — *BLUEBERRIES FOR SAL*
BERTA & ELMER HADER — *THE BIG SNOW*
CHARLOTTE ZOLOTOW — *SAY IT*
LEO LIONNI — *FREDERICK*

JOHNNY APPLESEED

FOR OPENERS

AS THE CHILDREN ARE COMING TO THE CIRCLE BEGIN TELLING THE STORY OF JOHNNY APPLESEED. "JOHN CHAPMAN ALWAYS LIKED THE SUN, ANIMALS, AND BEING OUTDOORS. WHEN HE GREW UP, HE DECIDED TO LIVE OUTDOORS AND DO SOMETHING NICE FOR OTHER PEOPLE. HE BEGAN WALKING THROUGH THE FIELDS AND FORESTS, AND OVER THE MOUNTAINS. (HAVE THE CHILDREN BEGIN WALKING IN A CIRCLE AS IF THEY WERE JOHNNY.) HE WORE A PAN ON HIS HEAD, (HAVE THE CHILDREN PUT BEANBAGS ON THEIR HEADS AS THEY WALK.) AS HE WALKED, HE TALKED TO THE ANIMALS OF THE FOREST. (LET THE CHILDREN PRETEND THAT THEY ARE TALKING WITH AN ANIMAL.) HE ALSO THREW APPLESEEDS EVERYWHERE HE WALKED. (HAVE THE CHILDREN TOSS 'SEEDS' AS THEY WALK.) HE HOPED TO TOSS ENOUGH SEEDS TO PLANT TREES SO EVERYONE WOULD ALWAYS ENJOY APPLES. PEOPLE BEGAN TO CALL HIM, 'JOHNNY APPLESEED'. HE LIKED THIS NEW NAME VERY MUCH."

FINGERPLAYS

TWO LITTLE APPLES

Way up high in the apple tree,
Two little apples smiled at me.
I shook that tree as hard as I could.
Down came the apples.
UMMMMMMMM! GOOD!

APPLE TREE

Here is a tree with its leaves so green.
Here are the apples that hang in between.
When the wind blows the apples will fall.
Here is the basket to gather them all.

SEPTEMBER

25

RECIPES

APPLE GOODIES

YOU'LL NEED

Apples
Peanut butter
Sunflower seeds or nuts

TO MAKE: Quarter and core the apples. Let the children cut the apple quarters into several slices. (Use table knives.) Spread the pieces with peanut butter, roll in seeds or nuts and eat for snack.

APPLE CIDER

YOU'LL NEED

6 cups apples cider
1 cinnamon stick
¼ t nutmeg
½ cup honey

3 T lemon juice
1 t grated lemon peel
18 oz unsweetened pineapple juice

TO MAKE: Heat the apple cider for about 15 minutes. Let the children drop in the cinnamon stick and other ingredients. Simmer for at least ½ hour. Serve warm or add ice cubes and serve cold. Enjoy for a snack.

FIELD TRIPS

● Visit an apple orchard. After the children have enjoyed picking the apples, let them take some home to their families.

● Walk to the grocery store and let each child pick out an apple. Buy them to enjoy as a snack at a nearby park. If the children picked out different types of apples, be sure to talk about the similiarities and differences in size, color, and shape.

LANGUAGE GAMES

EXPLORING
APPLES

Cut several apples in quarters. Pass the pieces around so all of the children have a piece. Ask, *"What do you see?"* Encourage the children to examine all around the apple. After discussing the parts of the apple, take out the seeds and eat the fruit for snack. Plant the seeds in small cups. Put them in the sun and water daily.

LANGUAGE GAMES

FELT BOARD FUN   Make two matching sets of different sized felt apples. Play a variety of games with them:

- Put one set of apples on the felt board. Ask a child to pick the largest; the smallest.
- Mix up the apples. Let the children put the apples in order by size. Begin with the largest and go to the smallest.
- Play APPLE MATCH. Put one set of apples on the felt board. Hold up one apple from the other set for the group to see. Ask a child to match the one you are holding to the one that is on the board. Continue until the two sets are matched.
- Scramble the two sets together. Let one child find one pair of apples. Then let another child find a second pair and so on until the two sets are matched.

ACTIVE GAMES

X ACTIVE APPLE   Have the children sit in a circle. As you play a record, have the children pass an apple from child to child. Stop the record. The child holding the apple leaves the circle and gets his/her snack. Continue playing until all of the children have gotten their snack.

BOOKS

ALIKI — *STORY OF JOHNNY APPLESEED*
JULIAN SCHEER — *RAIN MAKES APPLESAUCE*

SEPTEMBER

SUCCOT

FOR OPENERS

SUCCOT IS A HARVEST FESTIVAL. SUCCAHS ARE BRANCH HUTS OR BOOTHS. THE ROOF IS MADE OF BRANCHES, SO THAT THE PEOPLE INSIDE CAN SEE THE STARS. HAVE ENOUGH MATERIAL TO BUILD A SUCCAH FOR THE CLASSROOM. LET ALL OF THE CHILDREN HELP. PUT IT IN A PLACE WHERE THE CHILDREN CAN USE IT DURING FREE PLAY. DECORATE THE INSIDE WITH FRUITS.

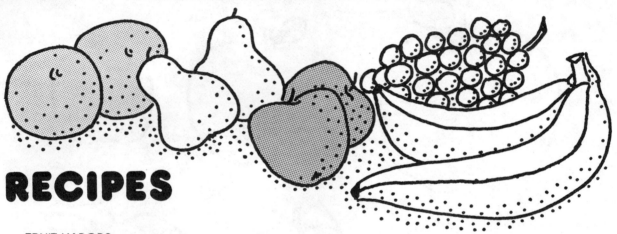

RECIPES

FRUIT KABOBS

YOU'LL NEED

Fresh fruits
Toothpicks

TO MAKE: Let the children clean the fruit. Cut the fruit into bite-size pieces. The children can then put two or three pieces of fruit onto each toothpick. Put on a plate and serve.

CARROT RAISIN SALAD

YOU'LL NEED

Carrots
Raisins
Walnuts
Mayonnaise

TO MAKE: Wash and peel the carrots. Let the children help the teacher grate the carrots. Put into a mixing bowl. Blend enough mayonnaise to hold the mixture together.

SUGAR COOKIES

YOU'LL NEED

All the ingredients for your favorite sugar cookie recipe.

Fruit cookie cutters

TO MAKE: Make your favorite sugar cookie recipe. Roll out the dough and cut into the shapes of different fruits. Frost the cookies with the appropriate color frosting.

FUN TO TRY: Make 'paint' frosting. Separate two eggs. Use only the whites. Separate the whites into 3 or 4 dishes. Add a few drops of food coloring to each dish. If necessary add a drop or two of water. Mix with a handmixer. With clean paintbrushes paint the cookies different colors.

LANGUAGE GAMES

FRUIT MOBILE — Make the crossbars for a large mobile. Let the children make pieces of fruit and bring them to circle time. As the teacher hangs each piece of fruit on the mobile, let a child name the piece of fruit and tell what color it is.

MEMORY — When children are sitting in the circle start the game by saying, *"Hanging in my succah is an orange."* All of the group repeat. The next child says, *"Hanging in my succah is an orange and an apple"*, adding another fruit to the list. All of the children repeat. Continue around the circle as long as the children can remember the sequence.

IN THE SUCCAH — Hang stars and a moon from the ceiling in the circle time area to give the children the feeling of night. Have all of the children lie down on the rug and pretend they are in a succah looking out at the stars. Have several children tell how many stars they can see. Let other children tell if they see the moon. Can anyone else see other things in the sky? What?

BOOKS

MARILYN HIRSH — *WHERE IS YONKELA*

OCTOBER

COLUMBUS DAY

FOR OPENERS

HAVE THE CHILDREN BRING THE BINOCULARS OR TELESCOPES* THEY MADE
DURING ART. AS THEY ARE COMING TO THE CIRCLE, BEGIN TEACHING THEM A
NEW SONG (TO THE TUNE OF ROW, ROW, ROW YOUR BOAT):

> SAIL, SAIL, SAIL YOUR SHIP
> SAIL IT NIGHT AND DAY
> LOOK FOR LAND, LOOK FOR LAND
> ALL ALONG THE WAY.

WHEN ALL OF THE CHILDREN HAVE GATHERED, ENCOURAGE THEM TO USE THEIR
BINOCULARS AS THEY SING. SING THE SONG SEVERAL MORE TIMES. AS A CHILD
SIGHTS LAND, LET HIM/HER POINT AND SAY "I SEE LAND." STOP THE SONG AND
LOOK WHERE THE CHILD IS POINTING. CONTINUE THE SONG AND LET OTHER
CHILDREN SIGHT LAND.

* Make a telescope or binoculars to bring to circle time. Decorate a paper towel
core or toilet paper rolls. (To make binoculars, let the children glue two toilet paper
rolls together.) Loop a piece of yarn around one end so that it will hang around the
children's necks.

LA GUAGE GAMES

Today we celebrate Columbus Day Christopher Columbus

TALK ABOUT Tell the story of Christopher Columbus. *"He was a man who thought the world was round and wanted to sail on the ocean to get to another land. He gathered some brave men together and received money from the King and Queen of Spain to sail three large ships called the Nina, the Pinta and the Santa Maria.* (Put three ships on the felt board.) *While the men were sailing on the ocean they were always looking for land. For many days all they could see was water.* (Let the children use their telescopes and binoculars to look for land.) *While they were sailing some of the men got sick.* (Ask the children why they think the men got sick.) *Finally one day a man shouted, 'I see land!' All of the men ran to see where the land was.* (Ask the children how the men felt when they finally saw land.) *Columbus steered the ships toward the land. When the men reached the shore, they all go off. They were very thankful."*

CREATIVE THINKING After telling the story of Christopher Columbus, pose this problem to the group, *"If you were on Columbus' ships and you ran out of food, what would you do?"*

ACTIVE GAMES

FOLLOW ORDERS The teacher is Columbus and gives orders to the sailors.

ROW THE BOAT!	*LOOK FOR LAND!*
PULL THOSE ROPES!	*RAISE THE SAIL!*
WASH THE DECK!	*QUIET, please!*

EXTENSION:
Let the children make up and give their own orders.

BOOKS

JANINA DOMANSKA — *I SAW A SHIP A SAILING*
JOHN BURNINGHAM — *MR. GUMPY'S OUTING*

OCTOBER

HALLOWEEN

FOR OPENERS

JUST BEFORE CIRCLE TIME, LAY A LONG ROPE IN THE CENTER OF THE FLOOR IN THE SHAPE OF A PUMPKIN. AS THE CHILDREN GATHER, HAVE THEM SIT AROUND THE OUTSIDE OF THE ROPE. WHEN SEVERAL ARE THERE, BEGIN GIVING COMMANDS, SUCH AS "STAND UP", "JUMP INSIDE THE PUMPKIN", "JUMP OUTSIDE AND WALK AROUND THE EDGE OF THE PUMPKIN". WHEN ALL OF THE CHILDREN ARE THERE, CONTINUE PLAYING THE GAME WITH THE ENTIRE GROUP. HAVE THEM HOLD HANDS AND "WALK" AROUND THE PUMPKIN (HOP, SLIDE, JUMP, TIPTOE).

FINGERPLAYS

SCARECROW

Scarecrow, scarecrow, turn around.
Scarecrow, scarecrow, see the ground.
Scarecrow, scarecrow, show your shoe.
Scarecrow, scarecrow, better say, "BOO!"

Scarecrow, scarecrow, get off your post.
Scarecrow, scarecrow, look for a ghost.
Scarecrow, scarecrow, look for a witch.
Scarecrow, scarecrow, she's in the ditch.

FIVE LITTLE PUMPKINS

Five little pumpkins sitting on a gate;
The first one said, "Oh my, it's getting late."
The second one said, "There are witches in the air."
The third one said, "But we don't care."
The fourth one said, "Let's run, let's run."
The fifth one said, "It's Halloween fun."
WOOOOOOOOOOOOOOO!!!" went the wind.
And out went the lights.
Those five little pumpkins ran fast out of sight.

THREE LITTLE WITCHES

One little,
Two little,
Three little witches
Fly over haystacks
Fly over ditches
Slide down moonbeams
Without any hitches!
Hey Ho
Halloween's here.

FINGERPLAYS

A WITCH

If I were a witch,
I'd climb on my broom
And scatter those ghosts
With a zoom, zoom, zoom!!

MR. PUMPKIN

Pumpkin red, pumpkin yellow,
He's a funny, funny fellow.
He's a jolly, funny sight,
Sitting on a post at night.

MY JACK-O-LANTERN

I laugh at my jack-o-lantern.
I think he is funny to see.
He must be thinking the same thing,
'Cause he's laughing at me.

RECIPES

PUMPKIN SEEDS

YOU'LL NEED

Pumpkin seeds
Salt

TO MAKE: Save the pumpkin seeds you've taken out of the pumpkin. Wash them carefully and let them dry. Put on a cookie sheet and bake at 325 degrees for about 10 minutes or until they turn golden brown. Take out of the oven and salt lightly. When cool, enjoy eating them.

PUMPKIN FACES

YOU'LL NEED

English muffins, bread or round crackers
Spreadable orange cheese
Olives, raisins, celery pieces, etc.

TO MAKE: Toast the muffins or cut the bread in the shape of circles. Let the children spread the cheeses and then make faces with the pieces of food you have made available. Enjoy for a snack.

EXTENSION: Make PUMPKIN FACES for lunch by decorating hamburgers with pieces of cheese cut in triangles, quarter moons, and circles.

ORANGE VEGETABLES/FRUITS

YOU'LL NEED

Carrots	Cantalope
Oranges	Sweet potatoes
Tangerines	Squash

TO MAKE: Fix the fruits and vegetables in different ways. (For example, you can serve the vegetables raw and cooked -or the cantalope with or without salt.) Talk about how they taste when fixed differently. Which do the children enjoy the most?

OCTOBER

33

FIELD TRIPS

● Enjoy a Halloween Walk. *"Fly"* through the air like bats. *"Ride"* on broomsticks like witches. *"Tiptoe"* like ghosts sneaking around the neighborhood. *"Flop"* like the scarecrows hanging on the post. *"Waddle"* like pumpkins.

LANGUAGE GAMES

CALENDAR
Start your PUMPKIN CHAIN so that the number of school days left before Halloween is equal to the number of children in your group. Depending on the children's level of skill, let each child trace around a simple pumpkin shape and then cut it out. Each child should decorate and have his/her name on the pumpkin. Cut strips of construction paper and fasten the pumpkins to form a chain. Each day during circle time, have the child whose name is at the bottom of the chain, pull his/her pumpkin off. As Halloween gets closer, the chain gets shorter. On Halloween Day the only pumpkin left will be the one that says, *HALLOWEEN IS TODAY!*

EXPLORING PUMPKINS
Have a large pumpkin sitting on newspaper in front of the group. Talk about what the children think is inside the pumpkin. Once they have had a chance to discuss what they think is inside, cut the pumpkin in half and the talk about the insides again. Is it what they expected? Next give each child a piece of newpaper and a wedge of the pumpkin. Let him/her *explore* it and save the seeds so that they can be eaten later.
EXTENSION:
During free play, cut another pumpkin into a *Jack-O-Lantern.*

FELT BOARD FUN ● Make duplicate sets of *jack-o-lanterns.* Depending on the group, make the faces very different or more similar. Put one set of *jack-o-lanterns* on the felt board. Hold up one face from the other set and have a child find the matching face on the felt board.

● Make a large pumpkin out of orange felt and put it on the felt board. Now cut up triangles, circles and other shapes that could be used for facial features. Let the children put the shapes on the pumpkin. MAGIC!!! They have created a large *jack-o-lantern.*

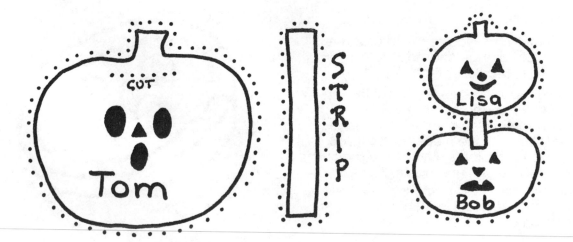

LANGUAGE GAMES

LISTEN CAREFULLY   Let each child pretend to be a ghost. Have him/her make ghost
                    sounds into the tape recorder. When everyone has been *spooky*,
                    play the tape back and guess who each ghost is.

CREATIVE   Have a ghost puppet. (Use white handkerchiefs, white gloves or
THINKING   mittens.) Put the puppet on and say *"Hi, I'm SPOOKY and I have
                    a problem. I hope that you will help me solve it. When I go to
                    children's homes on Halloween, they are always scared of me. I
                    am really a nice ghost. How can I make them like me?"* Let the
                    children express their thoughts.
                    EXTENSION:
                    Let a child, who wants to wear the puppet, tell a problem. Now the
                    other children can help solve it.

CREATE A STORY   The teacher should wrap a small piece of black felt around
                    "pointer" finger. That finger now becomes a *"witch"*. Tell the
                    children a story about a witch on Halloween.
                    EXTENSION:
                    Let the children add to the sequence of the story or let them
                    develop the ending for the story.

ACTIVE GAMES

WITCH PRACTICE   *"Witches, ghosts, goblins, bats, and black cats like to disappear and
                  appear again on Halloween. It is their favorite night of the year.
                  They need to get in shape to enjoy darting in between homes,
                  hiding behind garbage cans, flying among the stars, and around
                  the moon."* All of the children are witches and do what the *"boss
                  witch"* tells them. Choose a *"boss witch"* and start with exercises
                  like:

                      "Staying in the circle, run slowly."
                      "Swing your arms."
                      "Let's run in place."
                      "Tiptoe around the circle."
                      "Swoop around, going up — swooping down."
                  Remind the children to hold on to pretend brooms between their
                  legs while they are exercising.
                  EXTENSION:
                  Practice witch noises while exercising.

OCTOBER

35

ACTIVE GAMES

MUSICAL PUMPKIN   A variation of musical chairs. Cut an orange paper pumpkin for each child or get each child a small real pumpkin to use. Put the pumpkins in a large circle. Take one pumpkin out of the circle. Have the children walk around the circle while the music is playing. When the music stops, one child will not be standing in front of a pumpkin. This child should pick up one of the pumpkins from the circle and go to snack. The game continues until all of the children have a pumpkin and have gone to snack.

FIND THE GHOSTS   Make lots of tissue paper ghosts. Lay a white tissue flat. Put a piece of cotton in the middle. Gather the tissue around the middle and tie with a rubber band or piece of yarn. Just before circle time, hide the ghosts throughout the room. Play Halloween music and let the children search for the ghosts. When the music stops, the children should return to the circle.
EXTENSION:
When circle time is over, have markers available at the Art Center and encourage the children to put faces on the ghosts that they found.

BOOKS

ADRIENNE ADAMS — *THE WOGGLE OF WITCHES*
EZRA JACK KEATS — *THE TRIP*
ROBERT BRIGHT — *GEORGIE'S HALLOWEEN*
JANE THAYER — *GUS AND THE BABY GHOST*
ROBERT KRAUS — *HOW THE SPIDER SAVED HALLOWEEN*

THANKSGIVING

FOR OPENERS

THANKSGIVING IS A TIME WHEN EVERYONE TAKES A FEW MINUTES TO REFLECT ON ALL THE GOOD THINGS IN HIS/HER LIFE. WE TAKE THE OPPORTUNITY TO BE THANKFUL. IT IS ALSO A TIME WHEN MANY FAMILIES AND FRIENDS GATHER TOGETHER TO ENJOY EACH OTHER.

HAVE A LONG SHEET OF BUTCHER PAPER TACKED TO THE WALL. AS THE CHILDREN COME TO THE CIRCLE, BEGIN TELLING THEM THE STORY OF THE FIRST THANKSGIVING. WHEN FINISHED, LET THE CHILDREN THINK AND THEN TELL WHAT THEY ARE THANKFUL FOR. AS EACH CHILD SAYS WHY S/HE IS THANKFUL, WRITE IT ON THE PAPER. TACK THE LIST TO THE DOOR FOR EVERYONE TO READ. INCLUDE THE IDEAS IN YOUR NEXT PARENT NEWSLETTER.

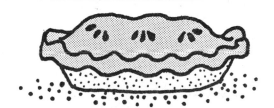

FINGERPLAYS

LITTLE PILGRIM

The brave little pilgrim
Went looking for a bear.
He looked in the woods.
He looked everywhere.

The brave little pilgrim
Found a big brown bear.
He ran like a rabbit
OH!! What a scare!

TURKEY GOBBLER

I met a turkey gobbler
When I went out to play.
"Mr. Turkey Gobbler,
How are you today?"
"Gobble, gobble, gobble,
That I cannot say.
Don't ask me such a question
On Thanksgiving Day."

THE TURKEY

The turkey is a funny bird,
His head goes wobble, wobble,
And all he says is just one word,
"Gobble, gobble, gobble."

THANK YOU

Mother, Father Sister, Brother,
Baby too will say,
"Thank you, thank you, thank you
On this Thanksgiving Day."
— HAPPY THANKSGIVING —

NOVEMBER

• Consider having a Thanksgiving Feast at the Center. Have the children participate in all of the preparations. A week or so before the Feast, have the children decide what they would like to eat. Once the menu is decided upon, then everyone should begin helping. Here are a few appropriate recipes.

RECIPES

APPLE CIDER

YOU'LL NEED

Apple cider
Cinnamon Stick
Orange peel

TO MAKE: Pour the cider into a large pan. Add a cinnamon stick and a little orange peel. Simmer for about an hour Enjoy the smell. Let cool. Drink before or during the Feast.

APPLESAUCE

YOU'LL NEED

Apples
Cinnamon
Honey

TO MAKE: Wash, cut and core the apples. Put a little water into the pan. Let boil and then add the apples. Cook over a medium heat until the apples are soft. Mash the apples. Add cinnamon and honey to taste.

GINGERBREAD

YOU'LL NEED

½ cup butter
¾ cup molasses
3 eggs
1 cup sour milk
2 cups whole wheat flour
¼ t ground ginger
½ t ground allspice
1 rounded t ground cinnamon
1 t salt
1 t baking soda
¼ t cloves

TO MAKE: Cream the butter and molasses together. Add the eggs and beat well. Measure all the dry ingredients into a sifter. Add dry and wet ingredients alternately. Mix well after each addition. Grease a 9" x 13" cake pan. Fill with batter. Bake at 375 degrees for 30 minutes.

from **COME AND GET IT**
by Kathleen Baxter

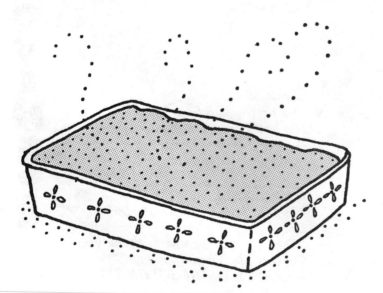

FIELD TRIPS

- Visit a turkey farm.
- Visit the zoo. Pay special attention to the turkeys.
- Walk to the nearby grocery store and buy the necessary food for the Thanksgiving Feast.
- Visit a nearby grocery store. Have the produce manager tell the group about the vegetables that are in season.

LANGUAGE GAMES

SORTING NUTS

Have different types of nuts (in shells) in a pile in front of you. Have the children look at the nuts. Hold one up. Have several children come to the pile and find all of the nuts that look like that one. Put them in an aluminum pie pan. Hold up another nut and let several other children find the matching nuts. Put these in another pie pan. Once all of the nuts are sorted, have the children carry the pie pans to the Discovery Table for further observation and examination during free play.

FOODS

Find pictures in magazines of foods before and after they are prepared. For example, fresh cranberries and cranberry sauce, raw carrots and cooked carrots, raw potatoes and mashed potatoes. Glue each picture to a piece of cardboard. Show the children all of the pictures. Then lay them out for everyone to see. Hold one of the 'before' foods up. Have someone find that food 'after' if has been prepared. When all the foods have been matched, point to each food and have the group whisper the name of the food.

NOVEMBER

LA GUAGE GAMES

FELT BOARD FUN — Make five Pilgrim people. Each should have a different expression on his/her face. Play a variety of games:
- Count the Pilgrims
- Talk about how the Pilgrims feel. Get clues from expressions on their faces.

- Make Pilgrim hats out of felt. Instruct the children to put the hats on the Pilgrims. For example, *"Pedro, put a hat on the fourth Pilgrim."*

CREATIVE THINKING   *"How do you show someone that you are thankful for all that they have done for you?"*

ACTIVE GAMES

SINGING   Sit in a circle and chant the following song:

RUN FAST LITTLE TURKEY

The brave little Pilgrim
Went out in the wood
Looking for a meal
That would taste really good.

First she picked cranberries
Out in the bog.
Then she saw a turkey
Hiding in a log.

Run fast little turkey.
Run fast as you may.
Or you'll come to dinner
On Thanksgiving Day.
      Dick Wilmes

(Change the pronoun for boy Pilgrims)

Have one child pretend to be the *Brave Little Pilgrim* and walk around the outside of the circle. As s/he stoops to pick the cranberries, have the teacher point to a second child who must get up and run around the circle before the *Pilgrim* can catch him/her.

PASSING THE PILGRIM HAT   Make a Pilgrim Hat. The children sit in a circle. One child sits in the middle of the circle and covers his/her eyes. Everyone sings the following song to the tune of *"ROW, ROW, ROW YOUR BOAT."*

Pass, pass, pass the hat.
Pass it 'round and 'round
Passing, passing, passing, passing,
Quickly 'til it's found.

While they are singing, the children are passing the Pilgrim Hat around the circle. When the song is over, all of the children put their hands behind their backs. The child in the middle opens his/her eyes and tries to guess who has the Pilgrim Hat.

GOBBLE, GOBBLE   The children sit in a circle. One child is selected *Parent Turkey.* S/he must leave the room. Several children are chosen *Baby Turkeys*. Have all of the children cover their mouths with both hands. The *Baby Turkeys* make a *'gobbling'* noise. When the *Parent Turkey* returns to the room, s/he must listen carefully and find the *Baby Turkeys.*

BOOKS

JANICE — *LITTLE BEAR'S THANKSGIVING*
ALVIN TRESSELT — *AUTUMN HARVEST*
LORNA BALIAN — *SOMETIMES IT'S TURKEY, SOMETIMES IT'S FEATHERS*
DARLOV IPCAR — *HARD SCRABBLE HARVEST*
LYDIA MARIA CHILD — *OVER THE RIVER AND THROUGH THE WOODS*
WENDE & HARRY DEVLIN — *CRANBERRY THANKSGIVING*

NOVEMBER

ST. NICHOLAS DAY

FOR OPENERS

BEFORE THE CIRCLE TIME, HAVE THE CHILDREN HELP SET UP AN OBSTACLE COURSE USING THE EQUIPMENT AND FURNITURE IN THE CLASSROOM. AT CIRCLE TIME, TALK ABOUT HOW ST. NICHOLAS TRAVELS FROM HOUSE TO HOUSE LEAVING "GOODIES" IN EACH CHILD'S SHOE.

"TODAY, WE ARE GOING TO PRETEND TO BE ST. NICHOLAS. BEFORE WE DO, HOWEVER, WE MUST ALL TAKE OFF OUR SHOES AND PUT THEM ALONG THE OBSTACLE COURSE." (LET THE CHILDREN DO THIS. WHEN THE CHILDREN RETURN, GIVE THEM A 'GOODIE' TO PUT IN THEIR OWN SHOE WHEN THEY PASS IT ON THE OBSTACLE COURSE.) "OK ST. NICHOLAS, IT IS TIME FOR YOU TO PICK UP YOUR SACK AND BEGIN VISITING ALL OF THE CHILDREN." (HAVE THE CHILDREN BEGIN MANUEVERING THROUGH THE OBSTACLE COURSE. HELP ANY CHILDREN WHO ARE HAVING DIFFICULTY. WHEN EACH GETS TO HIS/HER PAIR OF SHOES, HAVE HIM/HER DELIVER THE 'GOODIE'.) "OH! THERE ARE SO MANY CHILDREN TO VISIT. DON'T GET TIRED. ALL OF THE CHILDREN WANT YOU TO VISIT THEM WHILE THEY ARE SLEEPING."

AS THE CHILDREN FINISH THE OBSTACLE COURSE, HAVE THEM SIT BACK DOWN IN THE CIRCLE. WHEN EVERYONE HAS FINISHED, THEY MAY GET THEIR SHOES AND THE 'GOODIE' THAT ST. NICHOLAS HAS LEFT; RETURN AND ENJOY THE SNACK.

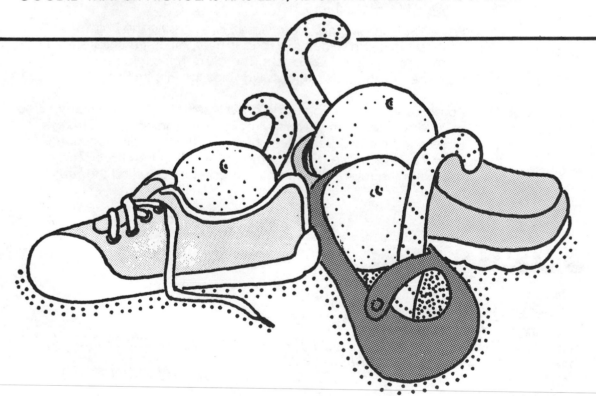

LANGUAGE GAMES

CREATIVE THINKING

"Pretend that you are St. Nicholas. You need to decide what gifts to gather for the children that you will visit. What presents should you put in your bag? What presents do you think the children would enjoy?"

FELT BOARD FUN

Cut several different sized sacks out of felt. Put them on the felt board. Point to one of them. Ask the children, *"What present could go in that bag? Why?"* Point to another bag. *"What would go in that bag?'* Continue until you have talked about all of the bags.

ACTIVE GAMES

SHOE SCRAMBLE

Have the children take off their shoes and put them in a pile in the center of the circle time space. The children should sit in a large circle around the shoes. Once the shoes are all mixed up, call several children's names. These children run to the shoe pile, find their pairs of shoes, take them back to their place in the circle and put the shoes back on. Quickly call several more children to find their shoes. Continue until all of the shoes are paired with the children.

GIFT HUNT

Get or make the same small gift for each child. For example, make a large batch of playdough and divide it into smaller portions for each child. Put each child's portion into a small plastic bag and tie a ribbon tightly at the top. If the children can recognize their name, write the name of each on the bags in large letters. If not, simply write "Happy St. Nicholas Day" on each one. Before circle time, hide the gifts. As the last activiy in the circle time, play some festive music and let the children hunt for their gift. As each child finds a gift, have him/her put it in a special place and go to the next activitiy of the day.

BOOKS

EVE RICE —*NEW BLUE SHOES*
MASAKO MATSUND —*PAIR OF RED CLOGS*
JEAN HOLZENTHALER —*MY FEET DO*

DECEMBER

43

HANUKKAH

FOR OPENERS

HANUKKAH IS AN EIGHT DAY FESTIVAL OF LIGHTS. THE MENORAH CONSISTS OF NINE CANDLES. THE CENTER ONE, CALLED THE SHAMMASH, IS USED TO LIGHT THE OTHER EIGHT, ONE ON EACH DAY OF THE CELEBRATION. MAKE A LARGE MENORAH WITH CANDLES OUT OF FELT OR COLORED PAPER. EACH DAY LET A CHILD ADD A YELLOW FELT OR PAPER FLAME TO ONE OF THE CANDLES. ON THE EIGHTH DAY, ALL OF THE CANDLES WILL BE BRIGHTLY "BURNING".

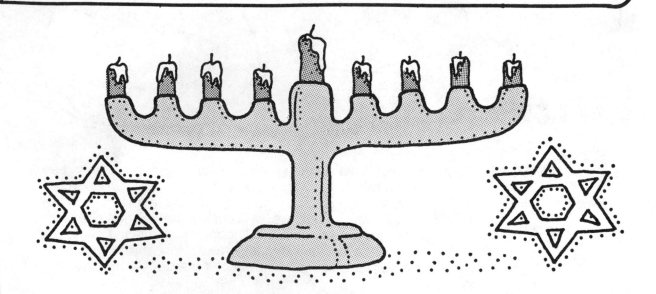

HANUKKAH SYMBOLS

Before the Hanukkah season begins, make this teaching aid to use throughout the holiday. Get a window shade and divide it into sections. Draw a symbol of Hanukkah in each section — Star of David, candles, Menorah, oil lamp, etc. Lay the shade in the circle time area and have the children sit around the edge of it. Use the shade for a variety of games.

- Introduce the children to the symbols. TALK ABOUT the pictures and what they represent.

- Once the children are familiar with all of the symbols, give them riddles. Describe one of the symbols and let the children guess which one you are talking about. The child who guesses the symbol can go and sit on that section. Describe another symbol and let another child guess which one is being described. Continue until all of the symbols have been talked about.

- Cut a piece of paper the size of one section. While the children are covering their eyes, put the paper over one of the symbols. When the children uncover their eyes, let them TRY TO REMEMBER which symbol is hiding.

44

LANGUAGE GAMES

PICTURES — Hanukkah is a family time when lots of pictures are taken. During art, let each child make a camera. Let the children collage materials onto a small box or block of wood. Have each child bring his/her camera to circle time. Have the children pair off and sit facing each other. Have one child pretend to take a picture of his/her partner. As s/he holds up the camera, have the child describe the color of the hair, eyes, clothes, etc. of the partner. Now switch roles and let the other child describe the appearance of the other. As the children are playing, walk to each pair and encourage as much language as possible.

ACTIVE GAMES

DREIDEL — A Dreidel is a four-sided top with a Hebrew letter written on each side. The children spin the Dreidel and see which letter turns up. As the top is spinning, the children chant:

I have a little Dreidel.
I made it out of clay
And when it's dry and ready
Then with it I will play.

Let the children take turns spinning the Dreidel.

BOOKS

DAVID ADLER — *A PICTURE BOOK OF JEWISH HOLIDAYS*
MARILYN HIRSH — *POTATO PANCAKES ALL AROUND*

DECEMBER

45

first day of WINTER

FOR OPENERS

BRING OUT THE SEASONAL CHART THAT THE CHILDREN BEGAN ON THE FIRST DAY OF FALL. READ ALL OF THE CHARACTERISTICS AND SOUNDS OF FALL. BEGIN TO TALK ABOUT THE CHANGES THAT HAVE OCCURRED SINCE THEN.

EXTENSION: WHEN TIME AND WEATHER PERMIT, TAKE A WALK AROUND THE NEIGHBORHOOD. ENCOURAGE THE CHILDREN TO LOOK FOR SIGNS AND LISTEN FOR SOUNDS OF WINTER. UPON RETURNING, TAKE TIME TO LIST THE CHANGES ON THE SEASONAL CHART. HANG THE CHART SO THAT EVERYONE CAN LOOK AT IT FOR A WEEK OR SO. SAVE THE CHART UNTIL SPRING.

FINGERPLAYS

SLEDDING

Here's a great big hill,
With snow all over the side.
Let's pull our sleds up to the top
And down the hill we'll slide.

WINTER WEATHER

Let's put on our mittens
And button up our coats.
Let's wrap scarves snugly
Around our throats.

Pull on our boots,
Fasten the straps,
And tie on tightly
Our warm winter caps.

Then open the door . . .
. . . And out we go
Into the soft and feathery snow.

MELTING SNOWMAN

Make three balls of soft, white snow,
Pat, pat, pat and watch them grow.
Big round snowballs, one-two-three,
Build a man of snow for me.
Sun comes out to warm the day.
Mr. Snowman melts away.

WHEN COLD WINDS BLOW

When cold winds blow,
And bring us snow,
At night what I like most,
Is to climb into bed
And hide my head
And sleep as warm as toast.

"Shhhhhhhh - Good Night Everyone."

46

RECIPES

SNOWCONES

YOU'LL NEED
Crushed ice
Juice
Small cups

TO MAKE: Make crushed ice. Let the children put some ice in each cup. Using small pitchers, let the children pour juice over the ice.

FROSTED JUICE

YOU'LL NEED
A Fresh coconut
Orange Juice

TO MAKE: Crack the coconut open. Let the children taste the milk. Scoop out the coconut and grate it.

Let each child pour himself/herself a glass of orange juice and then sprinkle some grated 'SNOW' on the top.

FIELD TRIPS

- Read the book, *THE SNOWY DAY* by Ezra Jack Keats. Then take the children for a walk through the snow. Give each child a stick or dowel rod so s/he can enjoy making tracks in the snow as the boy did in the story.

- On another day, take a walk in a different direction. Look at the trees. What has happened to them during the Fall? Are they all bare? Are some still green? What are the ones called that are still green?

- Hang a bird feeder outside of the classroom. Keep it filled with bird seed all Winter.

DECEMBER

LANGUAGE GAMES

TALK ABOUT   Discuss the different types of clothes that people wear in the Winter. Have pictures available for the children to look at and discuss. Ask the children if they wear the same type of clothes as are in the pictures.

EXTENSION:
Make winter clothes out of felt. Put the clothes on the felt board. Have the children name the clothes. Talk about the order in which the clothes are put on.

EXTENSION:
Have a felt body that the children can dress. While discussing the order of putting on the clothes, have the children come up to the felt board and dress the felt child.

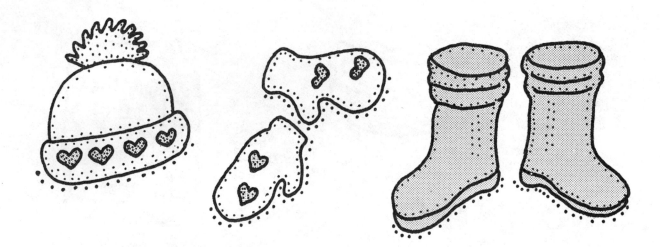

EXPLORING SNOW   Just before circle time let several children help get a bucketful of fresh snow. As each child comes to the circle, let him/her scoop some snow into an individual container and then sit down. Let the children smell, touch, and look carefully at the snow. Have small magnifiying glasses available. Talk about the snow.

EXTENSION:
Have the children bring mittens to circle time. After they have finished examining the snow, have the children get a bowl, put on their mittens, and build something with their snow. Let them keep the creation in front of them during the remainder of circle time. What is happening to the snow creations?

FELT BOARD FUN   Find pictures of all types of outdoor winter toys. Back them with felt and put the pictures of the toys on the felt board. Bring in as many of the real toys as possible and put them in the circle. First let the children name both the real toys and pictures. Then let the children tell stories about when they played with any of these toys.

EXTENSION:
After talking, play a matching game. Have a child come up, take one of the pictures off of the felt board, name it, and then match it to the real toy.

ACTIVE GAMES

CREATIVE
MOVEMENT

Let the children pretend to be *snowflakes* falling to the ground. Have one child pretend to be the *sun* and melt some of the *snowflakes* before they land. Have all of the *snowflakes* stand up and reach as high as they can. *"Snow falls very slowly and gently to the ground. It wiggles and blows in the wind.* (Let the children begin to fall from the sky.) *It is a very warm day and Mr./Ms. Sun is melting some of the snowflakes. If Mr./Ms. Sun warms you, simply melt away.* (Have Mr./Ms. Sun go around and gently touch several of the *snowflakes.* When touched, that child should pretend to disappear.) *Some snowflakes have melted, but others are landing gently on the ground. Soon the snow is covering the ground."*
EXTENSION:
Let the children discuss what they will play in the snow.

ICE SKATING

Have the children pretend that they are ice skating. While moving in a circle, have them glide, twirl, hold hands, tiptoe, glide backwards, maybe fall down, and so on. Remember: They are moving on skates.

SINGING

Sing *"FROSTY THE SNOWMAN."* After the children know the words, let them dance and march around as they are singing.

BOOKS

DECEMBER

EZRA JACK KEATS —*A SNOWY DAY*
A DELANEY —*MONSTER TRACKS?*
STEVEN KELLOGG —*THE MYSTERY OF THE MISSING RED MITTEN*
ALVIN TRESSELT —*WHITE SNOW, BRIGHT SNOW*
ALVIN TRESSELT —*THE MITTEN*
ELEANOR SCHICK —*A CITY IN THE WINTER*

ETHEL & LEONARD KESSLER —*SLUSH, SLUSH*
FREYA LITTLEDALE —*THE SNOW CHILD*
ROBERT WELBER —*THE WINTER PICNIC*
ETHEL & LEONARD KESSLER —*THE DAY DADDY STAYED HOME*

CHRISTMAS

FOR OPENERS

MAKE A LARGE SANTA CLAUS FACE. DIVIDE THE BEARD INTO TWENTY-FOUR SECTIONS. TALK ABOUT HOW CHRISTMAS IS GETTING CLOSER. HAVE A CHILD PUT A PIECE OF COTTON IN A SECTION EACH DAY. COUNT THE DAYS LEFT. WHEN SANTA'S BEARD IS ALL FULL AND FLUFFY, IT WILL BE CHRISTMAS EVE. THAT WILL BE THE NIGHT THAT SANTA CLAUS WILL VISIT EACH CHILD'S HOME.

VARIATION: MAKE AN ADVENT CALENDAR USING CHRISTMAS SYMBOLS, SUCH AS BABY JESUS, BELLS, CHRISTMAS TREE, CANDLES, GIFTS, AND SO ON.

FINGERPLAYS

CHRISTMAS PRESENTS

See all the presents,
By the Christmas tree,
Some for you,
And some for me.

Long ones, tall ones,
Short ones, too.
Here's a round one,
Wrapped in blue.

Isn't it fun
To look and see
All the presents
Under the Christmas tree?

CHRISTMAS TOYS

A ball, a book, and a tooting horn,
I hope I'll get on Christmas morn.

A ball to bounce, a book to read,
And a horn to toot quite loud indeed.

When I see Santa I'm going to say,
"Please bring these toys on Christmas Day."

I AM A TOP

I am a top all wound up tight.
I whirl and whirl with all my might.
And now the whirls are out of me.
So I will rest as still as can be.

THE CHIMNEY

Here is the chimney.
Here is the top.
Open the lid.
Out Santa will pop.

FOUR LITTLE BELLS

Four little bells, hanging in a row.
The first one said, "Ring me slow."
The second one said, "Ring me fast."
The third one said, "I'm like a chime."
The fourth one said, "It's Christmas Time."

HERE'S A BALL

Here's a ball,
And here's a ball,
And a great big ball I see.
Shall we count them?
Are you ready?
One! Two! Three!

JACK-IN-THE-BOX

Jack-in-the-box,
Jack-in-the-box,
Will you come out?
YES, I WILL!!!

FIELD TRIPS

DECEMBER

● Walk around your neighborhood and look for all of the ways that people are preparing for Christmas. Stop and look at the outside decorations. Talk about them. Have the children describe the decorations in as much detail as they can.

LANGUAGE GAMES

TALK ABOUT

Christmas is Christian holiday celebrating the birth of Jesus. A woman named Mary and a man named Joseph lived in Nazareth. They traveled to Bethlehem to register for the census. Bethlehem was very crowded when Mary and Joseph arrived. They could not find any place to stay that night. Finally they found a stable. Jesus was born in the stable. Ask the children *"What else do you think was in the stable with Mary, Joseph, and the baby Jesus?"* Give the children clues about the various animals that were also in the stable.

EXTENSION:

Soon after Jesus was born, shepherds and wisemen came to visit the family. They brought gifts to the baby. The shepherds brought sheep and the wisemen brought gold, frankincense, and myrrh. Ask the children *"Have you ever visited a new baby? (Let the children relate stories) Did you take the baby a gift? What gift did you take?"*

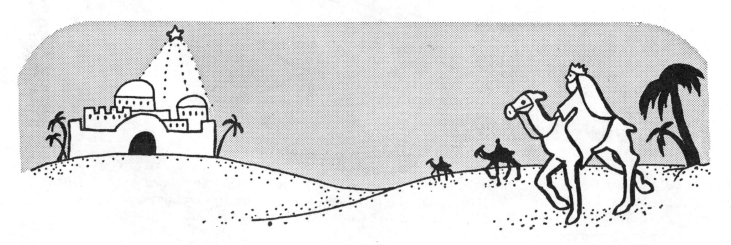

LANGUAGE GAMES

HAND PRINT TREE — At art time, have the children trace their hands onto different shades of green construction paper and then cut the hand prints out. Help the children, if necessary. Tell the children to bring their hands to circle time. On a large sheet of paper, help them arrange the hands in the shape of a Christmas tree. Glue all of the hands down. When dry, hang on the door for a holiday decoration.

CHRISTMAS WISHES — Have a long sheet of paper. During each circle time, have the children tell what they would like for Christmas. As each child tells his/her wishes, write them on the chart. Hang in the room for everyone to *"read"*. Add to it whenever a child has another wish.

DECORATING A TREE — During the day, make ornaments for the classroom tree. Let the children bring the ornaments to circle time and enjoy trimming the tree together.
EXTENSION:
Make a big bowl of popcorn. While everyone is decorating the tree, enjoy eating popcorn.

RIDDLES — Once the Christmas tree is decorated, ask the children riddles about the different ornaments. For example, say, *"I am looking at an ornament that is red, made of construction paper, has a round shape, and is linked to a green ornament. What ornament am I looking at?"* Let the children guess. If they need more clues, give them some more.

DECEMBER

LANGUAGE GAMES

IMAGINATION TREE Once the children have had the opportunity to decorate a tree and talk about it for a week or so, let them decorate one in their mind. First they should cover their eyes and imagine a bare tree. Ask them, *"Where is your tree standing?* (Let them answer)*Let's start decorating your tree. What is the first ornament that you are going to put on? What other ornaments do you want to put on your tree?* (Have the children tell you all about the decorations on the tree.)*Is there a special ornament on the top of your tree? What is it?* (Let them describe the decoration which they would like to put on top of their Imagination Tree.)*Let's put more decorations on your tree. Maybe something that is small and colorful and goes all over the tree. Maybe something shiny."* Let the children enjoy imagining all of the items which they would place on their Christmas Tree.

RINGING
THE BELLS

Get several bells that have distinctly different sounds. Ring them and talk about the sounds that they make. Which one do the children think might be used in a church? Which one might Santa use? Would reindeer wear any? As the group discusses the different sounds, let the children have the opportunity to ring them.
EXTENSION:
Put the bells on the Discovery Table so that the children can become familiar with the sounds. During another circle time, bring the bells back. Have the children cover their eyes. Ring one of the bells. Have the children open their eyes. Let one child pick which bell you rang. Have the child come up and ring the bell that s/he thinks was rung. Let the class decide if the rings sounded the same. Do this several times, using all of the bells.

TRY TO
REMEMBER

In the middle of the circle, have a variety of Christmas toys that the children would like. Name each toy. Then have the children cover their eyes. Take a toy away. Have the children open their eyes and try to remember which toy is missing. Name it.

54

ACTIVE GAMES

TOY CHARADE   Let the children pretend to be different toys. As a child is acting out the toy, have the other children try to guess what the toy is. If a child has difficulty picking a toy to imitate, the teacher should whisper a suggestion to him/her.

SINGING   Children enjoy singing Christmas carols. Here are several favorites. Add you own.

> *"RUDOLPH THE RED NOSE REINDEER"*
>
> *"JINGLE BELLS"*
>
> *"WE WISH YOU A MERRY CHRISTMAS"*
>
> *"RING, RING, RING THE BELLS"*
> *(To the tune of "ROW, ROW, ROW YOUR BOAT")*
> *Ring, ring, ring the bells.*
> *Ring them loud and clear*
> *To tell the children everywhere*
> *That Christmas Time is here.*

CREATIVE MOVEMENT   *"On Christmas eve, the reindeer will all gather in front of Santa's sleigh. They will fly through the air, land on rooftops, be very quiet, and then take off and fly again. Before the big night, all of the reindeer have to practice so that they will do it just right."* Let the children be reindeer and the teacher be Rudolph. Have the children form a *"line"* behind Rudolph. Each of the children holds the child's waist in front of him/her. *"Now take off and glide through the sky, land on the rooftops, be very quiet, wait for Santa Claus to finish distributing the gifts, and then takeoff again. Be sure to stop at all of the homes. Santa will be so proud of his reindeer."*

BOOKS

DECEMBER

ADRIENNE ADAMS — *THE CHRISTMAS PARTY*
JANICE — *LITTLE BEAR'S CHRISTMAS*
RUSSELL HOBAN — *THE MOLE FAMILY'S CHRISTMAS*
LORNA BALIAN — *BAH HUMBUG*
ROBERT KRAUS — *THE CHRISTMAS COOKIE SPRINKLE SNITCHER*
ROSEMARY WELLS — *MORRIS' DISAPPEARING BAG*

KWANZA

FOR OPENERS

KWANZA IS A HOLIDAY CELEBRATED BY BLACK AMERICAN FAMILIES FROM DECEMBER 26 TO JANUARY 1. IT CELEBRATES THE "FIRST FRUITS" TRADITIONAL OF AGRICULTURAL PEOPLE IN AFRICA. IT IS A JOYFUL TIME, A TIME WHEN THE ENTIRE COMMUNITY JOINS TO GIVE THANKS FOR LIFE, CROPS, AND EACH OTHER.

THE 'MKEKA' (PRONOUNCED MIKEKA) IS A STRAW MAT SYMBOLIZING THE FOUNDATION ON WHICH ALL OTHER THINGS REST. DURING THE FIRST CIRCLE TIME, HAVE THE CHILDREN MAKE A 'MKEKA'. GET STRAW FROM THE LOCAL GREENHOUSE, FLORIST, OR FARM. CUT LIGHT COLORED CONSTRUCTION PAPER INTO 4" BY 6" SHEETS. LET THE CHILDREN COLLAGE THE STRAW ONTO THE CONSTRUCTION PAPER. HAVE EACH CHILD PUT HIS/HER NAME (MAY NEED ASSISTANCE) ON THE MAT. PUT ALL THE MATS ASIDE TO DRY. WHEN THEY ARE DRY, TAPE THEM TOGETHER TO MAKE ONE LARGE 'MKEKA' THAT CAN BE USED THROUGHOUT THE REMAINING DAYS OF THE CELEBRATION.

CLASSROOM VISITOR

● Ask a person from the community who celebrates Kwanza to visit your class. Have him/her bring several of the Kwanza symbols to show the children. Discuss the symbols and the traditions of the holiday.

LANGUAGE GAMES

TALK ABOUT   On the last day of Kwanza, homemade gifts are exchanged. Let the children talk about gifts they could make for their parents and other members of the family.

FELT BOARD FUN   The *Kinara* (pronounced Vinara) is the candle-holder which holds the *Mshumma* (pronounced Mishumma), the seven candles. These seven candles represent seven principles: unity, self-determination, collective work and responsibility, cooperative economics, purpose, creativity, and faith. Three candles are red, three green, and one black. When the candles are put in the *Kinara,* the three red candles are on the left, the green on the right, and the black in the middle.

     Make the candle-holder and the seven candles out of felt. Put the *Kinara* on the felt board. Give the candles to the children. First talk about the red candles which mean struggle and blood. Let the children put the three red candles in the *Kinara*. Next talk about the green candles which represent youth, land, and new ideas. Let the children put the green candles in the *Kinara.* The black candle symbolizes unity. That candle goes in the middle.

FAMILIES   Have the children bring a picture of their family doing something together. Have a special bulletin board to tack all of the pictures on. Each day during Kwanza, let several children tell about their pictures. Encourage others each day to talk about things they like to do with their families. If their family is celebrating Kwanza, they can tell about the festivities.

ACTIVE GAMES

DANCING   Check out records of African music and dances. Ella Jenkins has several excellent albums which are appropriate for young children.

- Help the children identify the instruments they hear. If possible have several of them available for the children to use — drums, shakers, etc.

- Talk about how the music makes the children feel. Have them keep the beat by slapping their thighs, clapping hands, and/or snapping fingers.

- Cut two foot long red, green, and black streamers for each child. Have the children wave the streamers as they dance.

BOOKS

LEILA WARD —*I AM EYES . NI MACHO*
LORENZ GRAHAM —*SONG OF THE BOAT*

57

KINARA

DECEMBER

NEW YEARS

FOR OPENERS

NEW YEAR'S EVE AND NEW YEAR'S DAY ARE CELEBRATED IN MANY DIFFERENT WAYS. ONE WAY IS TO ENJOY A COSTUME PARTY. BEFORE CIRCLE TIME, HAVE THE CHILDREN FIND A COSTUME THAT THEY CAN WEAR. THEY CAN PUT ON DRESS-UP CLOTHES FROM THE DRAMATIC PLAY CENTER, FIRE OR POLICE HATS, OR SOMETHING THEY HAVE CREATED THEMSELVES. WHEN ALL OF THE CHILDREN HAVE GATHERED, LET THEM TELL WHO THEY HAVE DRESSED UP AS AND WHY.

HAPPY NEW YEAR!

LANGUAGE GAMES

TALK ABOUT   Discuss how the children and their parents will celebrate the New Year.

RESOLUTIONS   One thing that many people do at New Year's time is to make *"Resolutions"*, which are like promises. They are things that people would like to do in the coming year. What would the children like to do?
EXTENSION:
After each child has had the opportunity to talk about *"resolutions"*, get the tape recorder. Let each child say his/her *"resolution"* into the tape recorder. Play each one back and see if the children can remember who made that *"resolution"*.

ACTIVE GAMES

DANCING — Many people dance to celebrate the New Year. Give each child a colored scarf. Put on a favorite record and let the children dance and wave their scarves to the beat of the music. Select another piece of music with a different beat and let the children dance to this tune. Encourage the children to wave the scarves all around. Have them wave the scarves high and low, around their heads, in back of them, and so on.

FAVORITE GAMES — Some people play games at parties. Let the children have the opportunity to choose favorite games. Take time to play each game for a little while. Let the teacher pick the first one to get going. *"I know that we really like to play THE FARMER IN THE DELL."* After playing it, ask for more suggestions.

NOISE MAKERS — At midnight, people shout, cheer, and generally make a lot of noise to *welcome-in* the New Year. Many times there is a countdown to the stroke of midnight. Give each child a noisemaker or instrument. Begin at ten and count backwards. At zero, *welcome-in* the New Year. Do it several times! Children really enjoy making noise.

BOOKS

JANUARY

JANICE —*LITTLE BEAR'S NEW YEAR'S PARTY*

MARTIN LUTHER KING jr.

FOR OPENERS

AFTER MOST OF THE CHILDREN HAVE COME TO THE CIRCLE, BEGIN SINGING "HAPPY BIRTHDAY TO YOU" INSERTING MARTIN LUTHER KING, JR.'S NAME. THEN TALK ABOUT THE DIFFERENT WAYS THAT PEOPLE CELEBRATE BIRTHDAYS. LET THE CHILDREN TELL WHAT THEY DO ON THEIR BIRTHDAY.

HAVE A PICTURE OF MARTIN LUTHER KING, JR. EXPLAIN TO THE CHILDREN THAT HE WAS A MAN WHO HAD A DREAM. HE WANTED EVERYONE TO LOVE EACH OTHER. HE SPENT MOST OF HIS LIFE TRYING TO GET PEOPLE TO LIVE PEACEFULLY TOGETHER. HE WON ONE OF THE HIGHEST PRIZES A PERSON CAN EARN — THE NOBEL PEACE PRIZE.

FINGERPLAYS

I WISH

I wish I may
I wish I might
Have the wish
I wish tonight.

("_____ what is your wish?")

EXTENSION:
Make a felt star for each child. Pass the stars out just before you say the fingerplay. As the children are making their wish, have them put the star on the felt board.

RECIPES

First thing in the morning gather the children to make corn bread. Let the bread cool. At snack time sing "Happy Birthday" and enjoy the bread.

<u>CORN BREAD</u>

YOU'LL NEED

2 eggs
1 cup flour
4 T honey
1 t salt
2 cups yellow corn meal
2 cups buttermilk
1 rounded t. baking soda
2 T vegetable oil

TO MAKE: Beat the eggs. Add all of the other ingredients except the oil. When all is well blended, add the oil. Grease a 9"x13" pan. Bake at 425 degrees for 30 minutes.

from COME AND GET IT
by Katheen Baxter

LANGUAGE GAMES

TALK ABOUT

All people need to learn how to cooperate with each other. Talk about situations in the classroom in which the children could help each other — cleaning up, learning a new skill, reaching for something, helping to fasten a paint smock, etc.

CREATIVE THINKING

People need to live peacefully together. *"How do you show friends that you like them? What kinds of things do you do to let your family know that you like them? If a new child joins the class how could you welcome him/her?"*
EXTENSION:
"Two friends are fighting over a toy. They both want it. How can they solve their problem peacefully?"

ACTIVE GAMES

COOPERATION GAMES

Play several games in which the children need to cooperate:

- PASS THE BEANBAG: Have a beanbag. Start some music. As the music begins, give the beanbag to a child. Start passing the beanbag around the circle. Pass it carefully so it does not drop on the floor. When the music stops, the person who has the beanbag holds it. Start the music and begin passing the beanbag again. Continue playing until the song is over.

- WAVE THE PARACHUTE: Have the children sit around a lightweight parachute or double-size sheet. Have them hold the parachute with their fists on the top. Begin waving the parachute very slowly. If the children can do that in rhythm, have them do it a little faster and then faster, faster — STOP. Repeat several times.

EXTENSION:

It is also fun to wave the parachute while kneeling or standing.

BOOKS

NONNY HOGROGIAN — *ONE FINE DAY*
JANICE MAY UDRY — *LET'S BE ENEMIES*
CHARLOTTE ZOLOTOW — *MY FRIEND JOHN*
ELIZABETH CRARY — *I CAN'T WAIT*
ELIZABETH CRARY — *I WANT IT*
ELIZABETH CRARY — *I WANT TO PLAY*
MARGARET YOUNG — *THE PICTURE LIFE OF MARTIN LUTHER KING, JR.*
MARGARET BOONE-JONES — *MARTIN LUTHER KING, JR.*

CHINESE NEW YEARS

FOR OPENERS

THE CHINESE CALENDAR IS DIVIDED INTO 12 YEAR CYCLES. EACH YEAR HAS AN ANIMAL SYMBOL. MAKE CARDS OF THE 12 ANIMALS: SNAKE, HORSE, SHEEP, MONKEY, COCK, DOG, PIG, RAT, OX, TIGER, RABBIT, AND DRAGON. HOLD UP EACH CARD AND LET THE CHILDREN NAME THE ANIMAL.

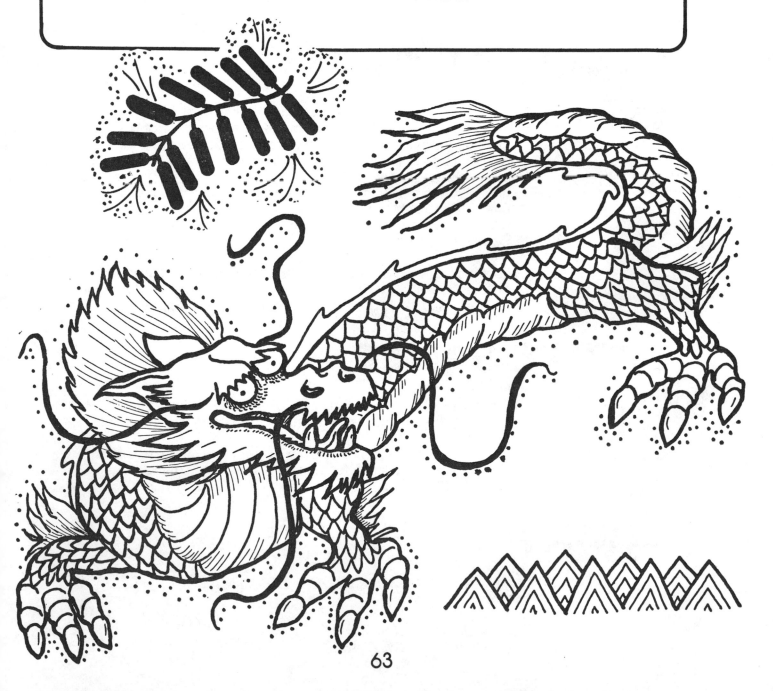

CLASSROOM VISITOR

Invite a Chinese parent into the classroom to talk about the Chinese people and how they traditionally celebrate the New Year. If your school does not have any Chinese families, talk to people of Chinese descent in the community. One of them would enjoy spending some time with the children talking about his/her culture and traditions.

LANGUAGE GAMES

TALK ABOUT
: The Chinese New Year celebration lasts for several days. Each day there are special activities including family feasts, neighborhood parties, and parades. One of the most popular events is the Lantern Festival. It includes a parade in which many families walk along carrying lanterns. The most exciting part of the parade is a huge Dragon made from paper mache and other materials. It is often so long and big that many people must help to carry it. The Dragon is a symbol of strength and goodness. As the Dragon passes, fireworks are shot off.

RED
: RED symbolizes happiness to the Chinese people. Encourage the children to wear red. Talk about all of the things in the room that are red. Ask the children what colors make them happy.

ACTIVE GAMES

HAVE A PARADE
: During art make Chinese lanterns. Take a walk around the school swinging the lanterns as if you were celebrating the New Year.
EXTENSION:
Draw a simple Dragon Head on a paper plate. Glue on a stick for the handle. Use a sheet for the rest of the body. Let the children take turns being the *dragon* leader.

BOOKS

DOROTHY VAN WOERKON — *THE RAT, THE OX AND THE ZODIAC*
LEO POLITI — *MOY MOY*
THOMAS HANAFORD — *MEI LEI*
RAYMOND CREEKMORE — *LITTLE FUN*
CHENG HOUTIEN — *THE CHINESE NEW YEAR*

GROUND HOG DAY

FOR OPENERS

WHEN MOST OF THE CHILDREN HAVE GATHERED, BEGIN TELLING THEM ABOUT THE GROUND HOG:

SOMETIMES CALLED A WOODCHUCK

MEASURES ABOUT 15" TO 18" LONG

HAS LONG FUR, USUALLY BLACK, GRAY, OR BROWNISH-RED

HAS SHORT LEGS AND A BUSHY TAIL

HIBERNATES IN THE WINTER

IS A VEGETARIAN

HAS A HOME CALLED A "BURROW"

FEBRUARY

FINGERPLAYS

THE GROUND HOG

A shy little ground hog left his bed.
He wiggled his nose and shook his head.

He looked to the left, he looked to the right.
The day was clear and the sun was bright.
He saw his shadow and ran in fright.

Then back to his burrow, he crept, he crept
And six more weeks he slept, he slept.

variation of poem by Marguerite Gode

RECIPES

Have the children help fix raw vegetables for snack. Pretend to be ground hogs while eating.

FIELD TRIPS

● If it is a sunny day, take a walk and have the children look for a friend's shadow. If it is not sunny, use the light from your projector or flashlight to let the children make shadows on the wall.

LANGUAGE GAMES

SEQUENCE STORY   Depending on the group of children, cut 4 (or more) 12" squares from lightweight cardboard. On each square, draw a simple picture of one part of the ground hog tale. For example: 1) The ground hog hibernating, 2) The ground hog coming out of his burrow, 3) The ground hog seeing his shadow, 4) The ground hog running back to his burrow. Lay the cards on the floor. Let the children put the cards in the correct sequence.

HIBERNATING

COMING out of BURROW

SEEING SHADOW

RUNNING BACK

BOOKS

CAROL COHAN — *WAKE UP GROUND HOG*
CROCKETT JOHNSON — *WILL SPRING BE EARLY?*

VALENTINES DAY

FOR OPENERS

CREATE A "FEELING TREE". MAKE A LARGE TREE OUT OF FELT. MAKE A HEART WITH A FEELING DRAWN ON IT FOR EACH CHILD. WHEN THE CHILDREN COME TO THE CIRCLE, HAVE THE BARE TREE ON THE FELT BOARD AND THE HEARTS IN A BOX. AS EACH CHILD REACHES THE CIRCLE, GIVE HIM/HER A HEART. WHEN ALL OF THE CHILDREN HAVE HEARTS, LET EACH ONE COME UP TO THE "FEELING TREE" AND NAME THE "FEELING" EXPRESSED ON THE HEART. THEN HANG THE HEART ON ONE OF THE BRANCHES.

EXTENSION: ON ANOTHER DAY, LET THE CHILDREN GET A HEART AND TELL ABOUT A TIME WHEN S/HE MIGHT HAVE FELT THE SAME WAY AS PICTURED ON THE HEART.

FEBRUARY

67

FINGERPLAYS

VALENTINES

Valentine, valentine,
Red, white, and blue.
I'll find a nice one
And give it to you.

(When the children know the words, give
each of them a small heart. As they say
the last line, have them give their heart
to the person next to them.)

VALENTINE'S DAY

Five little Valentines were having a race.
The first little Valentine was frilly with lace.
The second little Valentine had a funny
   face.
The third little Valentine said, "I love you."
The fourth little Valentine said, "I do too."
The fifth little Valentine was sly as a fox.
He ran the fastest to the Valentine box.

MY VALENTINE

Friends, I have quite a few,
But for my Valentine,
I CHOOSE YOU!!!

WHO FEELS HAPPY

Who feels happy, who feels gay?
All who do, clap your hands this way.

Who feels happy, who feels gay?
All who do, nod your heads this way.

Who feels happy, who feels gay?
All who do, slap your thighs this way.

(Continue making up your own verses.)

BE MY VALENTINE

Listen, Mother, I want you to know
Every day, I love you so.
As I throw you a kiss, Mother mine,
I want you to be my Valentine!!

(Use for dads, sisters, brothers, friends, etc.)

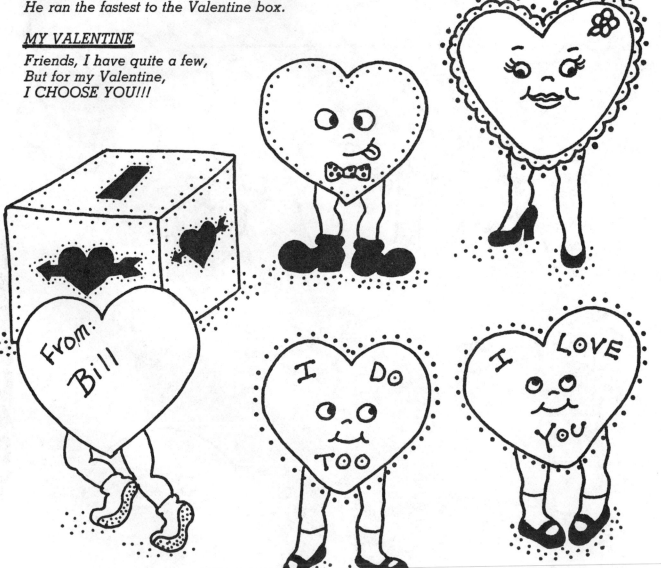

RECIPES

Let the children help you prepare and serve RED snacks during the Valentine holiday.

FRUITS

YOU'LL NEED

Apples
Strawberries
Cranberries

TO MAKE: Clean them and cut into serving portions.

JUICES

YOU'LL NEED

Tomato Juice
V-8 Juice
Cranberry Juice
Cran-Apple Juice

TO MAKE: Let the children pour the juice into small glasses for snack.

VEGETABLES

YOU'LL NEED

Radishes
Tomatoes

TO MAKE: Have the children wash the vegetables. Prepare them to the likes of the children.

FEBRUARY

FIELD TRIPS

● Have the children make Valentine cards for members of their family. Address and stamp them and then take a walk to the nearest mailbox. Each child should mail his/her own Valentine.

● Let each child make a Valentine card for him/herself. Help each child (or let them watch the adult) address the envelope with the home address. Then let each child carry the Valentine down to the Post Office. Have an employee of the Postal Service give the children a tour of the facility and explain how the letter will get to their homes. Then each child can mail his/her Valentine. It should arrive at his/her house within the next several days.

CLASSROOM VISITOR

If it is impossible to mail the Valentines outside of the Center, ask the letter carrier to stop in the classroom. When s/he does, have each child give him/her the Valentine. (Arrange this with the letter carrier several days prior.)

LANGUAGE GAMES

COUNT DOWN CALENDAR

Start your Count Down Calendar early enough to insure that each child in the group has at least one chance to participate. Make a heart for each day preceding Valentine's Day. Tape them to a long ribbon and hang it on the door. Each day let one child take a heart off and fasten it to his/her cubby. When all of the hearts are off of the ribbon, Valentine's Day has arrived.

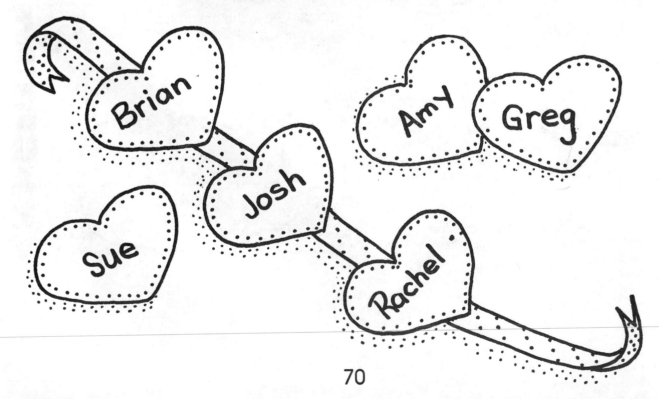

LANGUAGE GAMES

TALK ABOUT There are many ways that people show each other love. Let the children tell everyone the ways that their parents, brothers, sisters, and friends show their love. As the children share their thoughts, write them down. Hang the list in the classroom for everyone to enjoy.

POINTING OUT GOOD Valentine's Day is a day when people show each other how much they care and love one another. One way to let someone know how much you care is to tell that person all of the good things that you know about him/her. Take some time to talk about each person's strengths and what s/he likes to do. Discuss how each person is different and has certain abilities. Throughout the holiday, take opportunities during the circle time to think about and share the strengths and good points of each child.

VALENTINE CARD The teacher should make a Valentine card for each member of the class. Take a heart shaped doily and weave a piece of red or white yarn around the edge. Tie a bow at the bottom. In the center of the doily write *"I AM A VERY SPECIAL PERSON."* Place a circle of tape on the back. Give a Valentine to each child at the beginning of circle time. Let the children wear the Valentines all day.

FEBRUARY

FELT BOARD FUN Make a set of between 5 and 10 pairs of hearts and arrows graduating in size from very small to quite large. Put the hearts on the board. Let the children count them. Put the arrows on the board and count them. Now mix up all of the hearts and arrows. Ask a child to find a heart and arrow that go together. Have the child take the pair off of the board and hold it. Ask another child to find another heart and arrow pair. Hold that pair. Continue until all of the hearts and arrows are matched. Have the children come up and put all of the pairs on the board.

Make a large red heart and 10 small circles. Put the circles below the heart on the felt board. Count the circles. Let the children put a certain number of circles onto the heart. *"Greg, put 5 circles on the heart."* Everyone count aloud.

71

ACTIVE GAMES

PASSING OUT VALENTINES The day before Valentine's Day, have the children each decorate a bag. Tack the bags at the children's height along a wall or to a bulletin board. On Valentine's Day, have each child simply walk along and put a Valentine into each bag. When the children go home, they can take their bag full of Valentine cards with them.

SINGING Enjoy singing the following song:
> *One little, two little, three little hearts,*
> *Four little, five little, six little hearts,*
> *Seven little, eight little, nine little hearts,*
> *Bring love on Valentine's Day.*

LETTER CARRIER Pre-make red rectangles, circles, triangles, and squares. (At least one shape for each child in the group.) Put a Valentine sticker on each shape. Fold them in half or put in an envelope. Have the children sit in a circle. Choose one child to be the letter carrier. Fill a mail sack with the Valentines. The letter carrier gives a Valentine to each child. In turn, the child opens the card, holds it up, and tells what shape it is. Collect all of the Valentines and put them back into the mail sack. Let another child be the letter carrier. Once again the children can name the shape they receive.

FRIENDSHIP WALK All of the children sit in a circle. The teacher chooses a child to begin walking around the circle. As the child starts walking, the teacher begins to play a favorite record. When the music stops, the child picks the child s/he is standing near. When the music begins again, they hold hands and continue to walk. Each time the music stops, the children select the closest child to join them in their Friendship Walk. The game continues until all of the children are walking.

BOOKS

FRANK MODELL — *ONE ZILLION VALENTINES*
ADRIENNE ADAMS — *THE GREATEST VALENTINE'S DAY BALLOON RACE*
DAVE ROSS — *A BOOK OF KISSES*
DAVE ROSS — *A BOOK OF HUGS*

BLACK HISTORY WEEK

FOR OPENERS

AS THE CHILDREN ARE COMING TO THE CIRCLE, SING SOME OF THEIR FAVORITE SONGS BY ARTISTS SUCH AS ELLA JENKINS. IF YOU HAVE THE RECORDS, PLAY ALONG AS THE CHILDREN SING. (REPEAT THE SONGS OFTEN SO THE CHILDREN LEARN THE WORDS.) AFTER SINGING SOME OF THE SONGS, ENCOURAGE THE CHILDREN TO CLAP, SLAP THEIR THIGHS, OR SWAY TO THE RHYTHM.

RECIPES

Foods and recipes differ from region to region, but it is always fun to cook together. Yams can be prepared in a variety of ways.

YAMS

YOU'LL NEED
Fresh yams
Butter
Salt, pepper

TO MAKE: Have the children scrub the potatoes. Put them in boiling water. Cook them until they are tender. Take out. Peel, slice, and serve with butter, salt, and pepper.

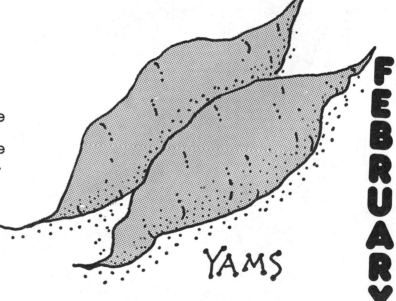

YAMS

FEBRUARY

FIELD TRIPS

● African people often make their own instruments by using the natural resources of their area. Check the library or museum for displays of African instruments. Make arrangements to visit the display.

73

LANGUAGE GAMES

TALK ABOUT

Cut out pictures of black families enjoying different activities. Give one picture to each child. Have the children look at their pictures. Those who want to, can stand, hold up their pictures, and tell the rest of the children what the family is doing.

EXTENSION:

Have pictures of black people involved in various occupations such as sports, music, education, construction, medicine, television, and so on. Talk about what these people do. Have a special bulletin board to tack the pictures on. After talking about each one, have a child pin the picture to the board. (May need teacher assistance.) When Black History Week is over, put all of the pictures in a scrap book and put the book in the Language Center for the children to continue to enjoy.

EXTENSION:

Use pictures of famous black people in history. Talk with the children about the contributions of these men and women.

LANGUAGE GAMES

SEEING YOURSELF   Give each child a mirror. While looking in the mirror, have each child tell one thing about what s/he sees, such as the color of eyes. After everyone has had a chance to say something, have the children look again and find something else.
EXTENSION:
Repeat this activity on other days, always encouraging the children to find something new about themselves.

MUSIC   Introduce a variety of music by current black musicians. Include African music. As the children are listening to the instrumental sections, have them identify as many of the instruments as they can. Have instruments available for the children to use.

ACTIVE GAMES

BODY MUSIC   Challenge the children to make body music. Find different ways the body can move to make noises, such as clucking the tongue and clapping knees together.

COPY CATS   Let one child clap out a rhythm with his/her hands. Then let everyone try to repeat it along with the 'leader'. Have the children take turns inventing rhythms.

FEBRUARY

BOOKS

DORIS SIMS —*STOP AND GO*
DORIS SIMS —*SUGAR MAKES SWEET*
DORIS SIMS —*SHOES GOT SOLES*
JOAN LEXAU —*ME DAY*
IANTHE THOMAS —*WILLIE BLOW'S A MEAN HORN*
IANTHE THOMAS —*HI, MRS. MALLORY*
EZRA JACK KEATS (ALL TITLES)

PRESIDENT'S DAY

FOR OPENERS

HAVE THE CHILDREN MAKE FLAGS AT ART AND BRING THEM TO CIRCLE TIME. AS THEY COME TO THE CIRCLE, HAVE THEM WAVE THEIR FLAGS AND SING, "HAPPY BIRTHDAY TO YOU", INSERTING THE NAMES OF GEORGE WASHINGTON AND ABRAHAM LINCOLN.

FINGERPLAYS

MY HAT

My hat, it has three corners.
Three corners has my hat.
If it did not have three corners,
It would not be my hat.

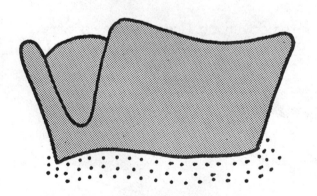

RECIPES

PRESIDENT'S PUDDING

YOU'LL NEED

Vanilla or tapioca pudding
Blueberries
Cherries

TO MAKE: Have the children help you make the pudding first thing in the morning. Just before snack, divide it into the appropriate number of servings. Sprinkle a few blueberries on each one and top with a red cherry.

CLASSROOM VISITOR

Contact the local historical society in the area. Ask a member to visit the classroom. See if the person who comes can bring pictures (or actual examples) of the clothes that the people wore during the time of Washington and Lincoln. Discuss the differences between then and now with the children.

LANGUAGE GAMES

TALK ABOUT   Make a miniature top hat like the one that Lincoln wore and a three-corner hat like the one worn by Washington. Fit the appropriate hat on your finger as you talk about each man.

<u>ABRAHAM LINCOLN</u>

He was a very tall and thin man.

His nickname was *"Abe"*.
(Talk about nicknames that the children in the group have.)

He liked to read books.

His wife's name was Mary.

He was President during the Civil War.

A man called John Wilkes Booth shot him while he and Mrs. Lincoln were watching a play.

<u>GEORGE WASHINGTON</u>

When he was a boy, he went to school every day. Not everyone went to school when he lived.

He liked to fish and swim.

He did not have a car.
(Let the children guess how he got around.) He had a horse whose name was *"Hero"*.

He was the first President of the United States.

His wife's name was Martha.

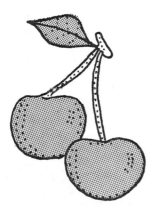

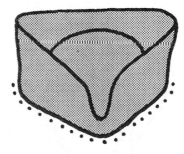

COLORS   Have the children wear red, white, and blue clothes this day. Talk about what the children are wearing. Have each child stand up. Let the other children look at him/her, and name the red, white and blue clothing that the child is wearing.

FEBRUARY

BOOKS

ALIKI — *GEORGE AND THE CHERRY TREE*

PURIM

FOR OPENERS

PURIM IS A HAPPY, NOISY JEWISH HOLIDAY. IT IS CELBERATED TO COMMEMORATE THE TRIUMPH OF THE JEWISH PEOPLE IN PERSIA. LONG AGO, THERE LIVED A KING NAMED AHASUERUS AND HIS WIFE ESTHER. THE KING HAD AN ADVISOR (MINISTER) NAMED HAMAN, A WICKED MAN, WHO PLOTTED TO KILL ALL OF THE JEWS. ESTHER'S COUSIN MORDECAI LEARNED OF HAMAN'S PLAN AND HAD ESTHER PERSUADE THE KING TO HELP SAVE THE JEWS AND TO GET RID OF HAMAN.

MAKE FINGER PUPPETS OF KING AHASUERUS, ESTHER, HAMAN, AND MORDECAI. TELL THE CHILDREN THE STORY OF ESTHER USING THE FINGER PUPPETS. AT THE END OF THE STORY, LET THE CHILDREN REJOICE AND MAKE LOUD NOISES OF TRIUMPH.

AHASUERUS

ESTHER

HAMAN

MORDECAI

RECIPES

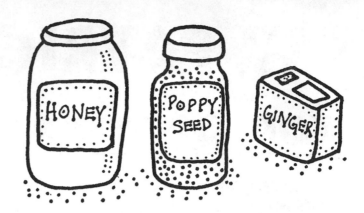

MONLACH
(A poppy-seed candy)

YOU'LL NEED

1⅓ cups of poppy seeds
1 cup honey
1 cup slivered blanched almonds
½ t. powdered ginger
cooking oil

TO MAKE: Grease a cookie sheet with the oil. Measure the poppy seeds into a sieve. Cover the seeds with boiling water. Drain and repeat one more time. Put the honey in a saucepan. Stirring constantly, bring the honey to a boil. Add the poppy seeds and almonds. Continue to stir until thick. Drop a spoonful on the greased pan. If the mixture holds its shape, stir in the ginger. Pour the mixture onto the greased sheet. Pat the mixture into a square about ½ inch thick. After several minutes, cut into small squares.

LANGUAGE GAMES

RIDDLES
Describe one of the characters in the Purim story. Let the children guess who it is. Describe another person. Continue until all of the characters have been guessed.

FELT BOARD FUN
Greggers or klappers are loud noisemakers used at Purim festivals. Make several solid color felt greggers for the felt board. Bring a lot of colored felt scraps to use. Put the undecorated greggers on the felt board. Pass the box of felt scraps around the circle and let the children take out several pieces. Now decorate the greggers. As the children put the felt pieces on the greggers, have them tell what color they are using.

ACTIVE GAMES

GREGGERS
Give each child a gregger. First talk about the colors of the greggers and how they work. Then play a listening game. One clap means make the greggers have a soft sound. Two claps means a little louder and three claps means a very loud noise. Practice the three sounds. Go slowly in the beginning until you are sure that the children understand the signals. When they understand, mix up the signals and go a little faster.

BOOKS

DAVID ADLER — *THE PICTURE BOOK OF JEWISH HOLIDAYS*
MEGILLAH, THE STORY OF ESTHER

FEBRUARY

ST. PATRICKS DAY

FOR OPENERS

LEPRECHAUNS OFTEN CARRY A BAG OF GOLD. BRING A BAG OF GOLD TO THE CIRCLE TIME. (IN A BAG, HAVE LARGE ROUND PIECES OF YELLOW CONSTRUCTION PAPER ON WHICH YOU HAVE WRITTEN THE NUMBERS FROM ONE TO TEN.) WHEN MOST OF THE CHILDREN HAVE GATHERED, BEGIN PULLING OUT THE "PIECES OF GOLD". LET THE CHILDREN SAY THE NUMBER ALOUD. ONCE ALL OF THE CHILDREN ARE THERE, GIVE A "PIECE OF GOLD" TO EACH CHILD. LET EACH CHILD TELL WHAT NUMBER S/HE IS HOLDING. AFTER THEY TELL, HAVE THEM PUT THE "GOLD" BACK IN THE BAG.

FINGERPLAYS

GREEN, GREEN

Teacher: *Green, green, green, green*
Who is wearing green today?
Green, green, green, green
Who is wearing green today?

Children (who are wearing green, stand up):

I am wearing green today.
I am wearing green.
Green, green, green, green,
I am wearing green.

WEE LITTLE PATRICK

Patrick is a leprechaun.
He has a sack of gold.
He hides it in a special place
Between two stumps, I'm told.

I think I once saw Patrick
Out in the woods at play.
He smiled and laughed and winked his eye,
And then he ran away.

Don't try to follow Patrick
To find his treasure sack.
He'll twist and jump and run away
And never will come back.
Dick Wilmes

RECIPES

VEGETABLE TRAY

YOU'LL NEED

Celery - Green Peppers - Broccoli
Spinach - Green Beans - Lettuce
and other green vegetables.

TO MAKE: Have the children wash the vegetables and arrange them on a tray. Make a vegetable dip. Keep everything in the refrigerator until snacktime.

LANGUAGE GAMES

SORTING
THE CHIPS
Get different shades of green paint chips from the paint store. Lay them on the floor for everyone to see. Ask the group, *"Which chip is the lightest green?"* Have someone point to it. Put tape on the back of the chip and stick it to a piece of posterboard. Have the children find the next lightest paint chip. Tape it next to the first one. Continue until the children have sorted the colors from the lightest to the darkest green.

GREEN WATER
Have a glass of clear water and green food coloring. Talk about what color the water is. (Probably clear or no color.) Add a little bit of green food coloring. Watch what happens. Have the children describe what is happening to the water. After it is all diffused, discuss what color the water is. *"Light green."* Add a little more food coloring. Continue until the water has changed to *"Dark green."*
VARIATION:
Instead of using the same glass of water and adding more and more food coloring each time, use several different glasses and add more food coloring to each successive glass of water. When finished, the water in the glasses will range from light to dark green.

ACTIVE GAMES

HIDDEN
SHAMROCKS

Pre-cut about thirty shamrocks. Just before circle time carefully hide the shamrocks around the room or outside if warm enough. Tell the children that there are shamrocks hiding all around. When the music begins, (Have some Irish music.) they can begin looking for them. When the music stops, they should all return to the circle.

BOOKS

ELIZABETH SHUB —*SEEING IS BELIEVING*
LORNA BALIAN —*LEPRECHAUNS NEVER LIE*
EVE BUNTING —*ST. PATRICK'S DAY IN THE MORNING*

first day of SPRING

FOR OPENERS

MANY BABY ANIMALS ARE BORN IN SPRINGTIME. COLLECT ENOUGH PICTURES OF BABY ANIMALS SO THAT EACH CHILD AT YOUR CIRCLE TIME WILL BE ABLE TO HAVE A TURN. HOLD THE PICTURES UP ONE AT A TIME AND LET THE CHILDREN IDENTIFY THE BABY ANIMALS. ONCE THE CHILDREN KNOW THE NAMES OF ALL THE BABIES, PASS OUT THE PICTURES AND DESCRIBE ONE OF THE ANIMALS. THE CHILD WHO IS HOLDING THE PICTURE OF THAT ANIMAL SHOULD STAND UP AND SAY, "I HAVE THE _____". WHEN ALL OF THE CHILDREN ARE STANDING WITH A PICTURE, GO AROUND THE CIRCLE AND IDENTIFY THE ANIMALS ONE MORE TIME. HAVE THE FIRST CHILD HOLD UP THE ANIMAL PICTURE AND LET THE REST OF THE CHILDREN SAY WHICH ANIMAL IT IS. THEN HAVE THE CHILD GIVE THE PICTURE TO YOU. COLLECT ALL OF THE ANIMAL PICTURES IN THIS WAY.

FINGERPLAYS

A ROBIN

When a robin cocks his head
Sideways in a flower bed,
He can hear the tiny sound
Of a worm beneath the ground.

SPRING

Now put away your sled,
Take off your warm red mittens.
For pussy willow's out today
With all her soft gray kittens.

PITTER PATTER

Pitter, patter falls the rain
On the roof and window pane.
Softly, softly it comes down
Makes a stream that runs around.

RAIN

Rain on the green grass
And rain on the tree,
Rain on the roof top,
But not on me.

FINGER PLAYS

FIVE LITTLE DUCKS

Five little ducks, that I once knew,
Fat one, skinny one, tall ones two.
But the one little duck
With the feather on his back,
He led the others
With a "Quack, Quack, Quack.
Quack, Quack, Quack!"

Down to the river they would go,
Wibble, wabble, wibble, wabble
  to and fro
But the one little duck
With the feather on his back,
He led the others
With a "Quack, Quack, Quack.
Quack, Quack, Quack!"

Up from the river they would come.
Ho, ho, ho, ho, hum, hum, hum
But the one little duck
With the feather on his back,
He led the others
With a "Quack, Quack, Quack.
Quack, Quack, Quack!"

RAINY DAY FUN

Slip on your raincoat
Pull on galoshes
Wading in puddles
Make splishes and sploshes!

DIG A LITTLE HOLE

Dig a little hole.
Plant a little seed.
Pour a little water.
Pull a little weed.

Chase a little bug.
Heigh-ho there he goes!
Give a little sunshine.
Grow a little rose.

SAFETY

Red says STOP.
And green says GO.
Yellow says CAUTION,
You'd better go slow!

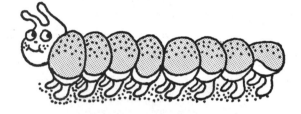

THE CATERPILLAR

A caterpillar crawled to the top of the tree.
"I think I'll take a nap," said he.
So - under a leaf he began to creep,
To spin his cocoon and fall asleep.
All Winter he slept in his cocoon bed,
Til Spring came along one day and said,
"Wake up, wake up, little sleepy head.
Wake up, it's time to get out of your bed."
So — he opened his eyes that sun shiny day.
Lo! He was a butterfly and he flew away.

MARCH

FIELD TRIPS

● Take a walk. Look for signs and listen for sounds of Spring. Upon returning, take out the Seasonal Chart. Read the different characteristics of Fall and Winter. Now add Spring to the Chart.

● Take a walk on a windy day. Give each child a scarf or streamer. As they walk, they can hold it up and watch what the wind does with it. Have them hang on tightly. Carry extras in case a child lets go.

● Take a trip to a nearby zoo or farm. Enjoy all of the baby animals that have been born this Spring.

LANGUAGE GAMES

TALK ABOUT   Discuss all of the signs of Spring with the children: A time of rain, of buds on the trees, of flowers beginning to grow, of snow gone, of light-weight clothes, of animals shedding their winter coats, of hibernating animals waking up, of farmers planting, of baby animals being born. Add more to the list depending on your part of the country.

PLANTING   Spring is a time for planting. Some people plant flowers and small gardens, farmers plant fields with crops, and the wind spreads seeds through the air to land someplace and plant themselves. Take the opportunity to plant various seeds with the children. Let them choose what they would like to grow. After planting, establish a schedule for caring for the plants.

EXTENSION:

Sprouts are good seeds to grow, because it only takes a couple of days to see the results. Cover the bottom of a glass jar with ¼ inch of seeds. Cover the mouth of the jar with a piece of cheesecloth and secure with rubber bands. Pour cool water through the cheesecloth, rinse and drain. Cover the seeds with warm water and let soak overnight. In the morning, drain off the water, rinse with lukewarm water and drain again thoroughly. Continue to rinse once or twice a day for 3 or 4 days or until the sprouts are the desired length.

FELT BOARD FUN   • Make feltboard pieces that show the growth of a flower seed. Have a seed, roots, stem, leaves, and flower. (Make other examples depending on the type of vegetation, plants, and flowers in your area.) Put the parts of the flower on the felt board. Talk about each part. Have the children come to the board and put the appropriate part onto the growing flower.

• Find pairs of pictures of baby and adult animals. Back the pictures with felt. Scramble the pictures on the felt board. Let children take turns matching the baby to the adult animal and vice versa.

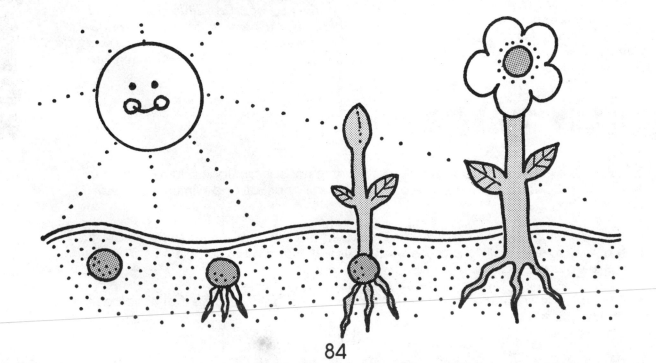

ACTIVE GAMES

CREATIVE MOVEMENT

Have the children begin as *seeds* being planted and grow into brightly colored flowers. *"It is Spring and time to do the planting. After the ground has been prepared, holes are dug to put the seeds in.* (Have the children kneel down and curl up like a seed.) *During the next weeks, the warm sun heats the ground and seeds. Water brings nourishment. Soon a root begins to grow and wiggles through the soil.* (Have the children begin to uncurl.) *Soon a stem begins to come through the ground and grows tall.* (Have the children squat.) *Leaves sprout out and the stem continues to grow.* (The arms can be leaves and the children can be almost standing up straight.) *The warm sun and rain continue to help the flower grow. Soon a bud is on the flower and it begins to open up.* (Have the children stand straight with their heads tucked down.) *The bud blooms and the flower looks beautiful."* (Have all of the children stand straight up, arms out, and heads up with bright smiles on their faces.)

ANIMAL FROLIC

Young animals love to romp. Pretend to be different animals moving around — Kangaroos, hop; fish, swim; lions, stalk; birds, fly; worms, wiggle; ducks, waddle; and so on.

SAFETY MARCH

The teacher holds three circles — red, yellow, and green. The children begin marching around the circle. When the teacher holds up the *RED light,* everyone must stop. Continue marching on the *GREEN light.* Stop and look around when the *YELLOW light* appears, and then do whatever the next *light* says.

BOOKS

MARCH

ERIC CARLE — *THE VERY HUNGRY CATERPILLAR*
LEO LIONNI — *INCH BY INCH*
GENE ZION — *REALLY SPRING*
MARIE HALL ETS — *GILBERTO AND THE WIND*
LUCILLE CLIFTON — *THE BOY WHO DIDN'T BELIEVE IN SPRING*

85

PASSOVER

FOR OPENERS

PASSOVER IS A FESTIVAL OF FREEDOM. IT IS A RELIGIOUS HOLIDAY CELEBRATED BY JEWISH PEOPLE COMMEMORATING THE TIME WHEN MOSES LEAD THE ISRAELITES TO FREEDOM. BECAUSE THE PEOPLE DID NOT HAVE TIME TO PACK THEIR BELONGINGS AND FOOD FOR THE JOURNEY, THEY QUICKLY MADE AN UNLEAVENED MEAL WHICH THEY COULD USE LATER TO MAKE BREADS. THIS MEAL IS CALLED "MATZO" WHICH MEANS "UNLEAVENED."

FAMILIES CELEBRATE PASSOVER BY JOINING TOGETHER FOR THE SEDER DINNER. TO PREPARE FOR THE MEAL, ALL GRAIN IS REMOVED FROM THE HOUSE AND THE HOME IS THOROUGHLY CLEANED.

OFTENTIMES DRIED FRUITS ARE SERVED AT THE SEDER. HAVE A VARIETY OF DRIED AND FRESH FRUITS FOR THE CHILDREN TO TASTE AND COMPARE. FOR EXAMPLE DRIED AND FRESH APRICOTS, APPLES, PINEAPPLES, COCONUTS AND RAISINS/GRAPES. TALK ABOUT THE TASTE AND TEXTURE DIFFERENCES BETWEEN THE DRIED AND FRESH FRUITS.

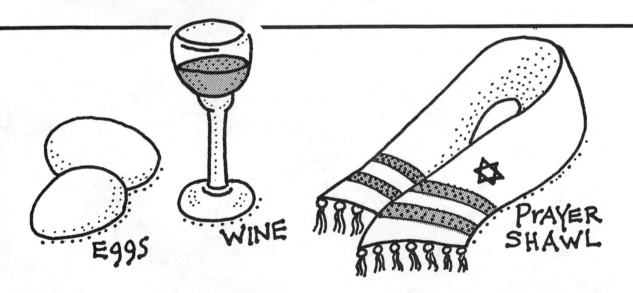

EGGS WINE PRAYER SHAWL

CLASSROOM VISITOR

Ask a Jewish parent or local rabbi to visit the class and tell the children about this holiday. If s/he has pictures or slides of the Seder, ask him/her to show the children.

LANGUAGE GAMES

PASSOVER SYMBOLS   Get a double bed sheet. Using tempera paint, draw a large circle on the sheet and divide it into as many sections as you have children in your group. In each section, paint a picture of a Passover symbol or one of the Seder foods. Make a card to match each of the symbols. Have the children sit around the sheet. Give each child a card. Then describe one of the symbols. The child who has that symbol should stand up, say the name of the symbol, and put the card on the matching section of the sheet. Continue
EXTENSION:
Hold hands and walk around the sheet. Softly ring a bell as a signal to stop. Let the children name the symbol that they are standing near. Continue for several more times.

TALK ABOUT   Everyone eats a piece of the Afikkomen at the conclusion of the Seder dinner. This is for *"good luck."* Discuss what the children think "good luck" means.

ACTIVE GAMES

CLEANING   For several days before Passover, use the circle time period to clean the classroom. Give the children tasks each day, such as dusting, sweeping, washing tables, straightening shelves, etc.

AFIKKOMEN   One of the children's favorite Passover traditions is the treasure hunt that happens at the conclusion of the Seder dinner. The father wraps a special piece of matzo called Afikkomen and hides it. The children search for it. The child who finds the Afikkomen brings it back to the father and s/he gets a reward. Then everyone tastes the Afikkomen for *"good luck."* Have a treasure hunt during circle time.

BOOKS

MARILYN HIRSCH — *ONE LITTLE GOAT*
URI SHULEVITZ — *THE MAGICIAN*

APRIL FOOLS DAY

FOR OPENERS

APRIL FIRST IS A DAY FOR PLAYING TRICKS AND GAMES. "WHAT HAPPENS WHEN SOMEBODY PUTS AIR INTO A BALLOON?" HAVE A BALLOON AND BLOW IT UP. "WHAT DO BALLOONS DO WHEN YOU LET THE BALLOON FREE?" LET GO OF THE BALLOON THAT YOU HAVE JUST BLOWN UP. NOW LET THE CHILDREN PRETEND THAT THEY ARE BALLOONS. DISCUSS WHAT COLOR AND SHAPE OF BALLOON EACH CHILD WANTS TO BE. AS YOU BEGIN TO BLOW, THE "BALLOONS" GET BIGGER AND BIGGER UNTIL THEY ARE ALL BLOWN UP. QUICKLY WALK AROUND THE CIRCLE AND LET EACH "BALLOON" GO FREE SO THAT IT CAN FIZZLE AROUND THE ROOM AND GLIDE TO THE FLOOR. NEXT LET THE CHILDREN PRETEND TO BE A DIFFERENT COLOR AND SHAPE OF BALLOON. BEGIN TO BLOW THE "BALLOONS" UP JUST AS BEFORE AND LET THEM FLY AROUND AS THEY SWOOP BACK TO THE FLOOR.

FINGERPLAYS

APRIL FIRST

Little bears have three feet.
Little birds have four.
Little cows have two feet.
Girls and boys have more.

Do you believe my story?
Do you believe my song?
I'll tell it only once a year.
When April comes along.
— APRIL FOOL —

WIND TRICKS

The wind is full of tricks today,
He blew my daddy's hat away.
He chased our paper down the street.
He almost blew us off our feet.
He makes the trees and bushes dance.
Just listen to him howl and prance.

APRIL TRICKERY

The big round sun in an April sky,
Winked at a cloud that was passing by.
The grey cloud laughed as it scattered rain.
Then out came the big round sun again.

88

RECIPES

INSIDE-OUT SNACK

YOU'LL NEED

Cheese
Crackers

TO MAKE: Put a cracker between two pieces of cheese. Enjoy these *"inside-out snacks"* with your children.

MONKEY MEAL

YOU'LL NEED

Hot dog buns
Peanut butter
Bananas

TO MAKE: Peel the bananas. Spread peanut butter in the bun and put in a banana. Cut the *"monkey meals"* in half and serve.

MONKEY MEAL

CLASSROOM VISITOR

Contact the dramatics coordinator at your local community college or high school to see if there is a clown or magician that will visit your class.

LANGUAGE GAMES

LISTEN AND THINK   Make statements to the children — some silly, some serious. They say *"Yes"* or *"No"* depending on the statement you make. Begin by saying, *"I'm going to try to fool you, so listen carefully. Say, 'Yes' or 'No' to my statements."*

> *"Dogs like donuts and coffee."* — Noooo!
>
> *"I can put an elephant in my pocket."* — Noooo!
>
> *"You eat dinner in the morning."* — Noooo!
>
> *"A tiger is an animal."* — Yessss!

LANGUAGE GAMES

SILLY PICTURES   Make large silly April Fool pictures by mixing various parts of animals, foods, furniture, people, and transportation. Show the pictures to the children. Have them identify the different parts. Maybe they can even think of names for the silly pictures.

ACTIVE GAMES

STOP AND GO   Have the children all get behind a starting line. Stand about 15 feet away from the children, facing them. When you say *"GO"*, the children walk as fast as they can towards you. When you say *"STOP"*, the children stop as fast as they can. When all of the children finally reach you, play again and let one of the children be the leader.

FREEZE   In this game, the music will try to "trick" the children. Start the record. While the children hear the music, they should dance. When the music stops, the children should stop in whatever position they are in.

BOOKS

FERNANDO KRAHN — *APRIL FOOLS*
EZRA JACK KEATS — *GOGGLES*
PAUL GALDONE — *THREE SILLIES*

EASTER

FOR OPENERS

HAVE AN EASTER BUNNY PUPPET AND A LARGE EASTER BASKET. GIVE EACH CHILD SEVERAL PLASTIC EGGS OR SOME MADE FROM WALLPAPER. HAVE THE EASTER BUNNY DO THE TALKING. HE IS LOOKING FOR HIS EGGS TO TAKE TO THE BOYS AND GIRLS. "HELLO BOYS AND GIRLS. I'M PETER AND I'M LOOKING FOR ALL OF MY EGGS. I HOPE THAT YOU CAN HELP ME." THEN BEGIN DESCRIBING DIFFERENT EGGS. AS PETER DESCRIBES THE EGGS, HAVE THE CHILREN BRING THEM UP. "I AM LOOKING FOR A PLAIN YELLOW EGG. (A CHILD BRINGS IT UP.) THANK YOU. NOW I WANT A WHITE EGG WITH A RED STRIPE." CONTINUE UNTIL PETER'S BASKET IS FULL AND THE CHILDREN HAVE NO MORE EGGS.

FINGERPLAYS

EASTER BUNNY

Easter Bunny's ears are floppy.
Easter Bunny's feet are hoppy.
His fur is soft and his nose is fluffy,
Tail is short and powder-puffy.

A FAT BUNNY

A fat bunny rabbit with ears so tall,
And two pink eyes about this small,
When hop, hop, hopping to get some lunch.
He found a fresh carrot,
A yum-yum. Crunch, crunch!

THE FUNNY BUNNY

Here is a bunny
With ears so funny.
Here is his hole in the ground.
He hears a noise and perks up his ears.
He jumps into his hole in the ground.

APRIL

91

RECIPES

DYEING EASTER EGGS

YOU'LL NEED

Beets - deep red
Yellow onions - yellow
Cranberries - light red
Spinach leaves - green
Blackberries - blue

TO MAKE: Pick 2 or 3 colors from the list above. Make several natural dyes by boiling fruits or vegetables in small amounts of water. Let the children put a cool hard boiled egg in a nylon stocking and dip it into the dye. Keep the egg in the dye for several minutes. Pull out the nylon and check the color. If dark enough, put on a paper towel to dry.

FIELD TRIPS

● Hatch chicken eggs. Contact a hatchery in your area where you can buy the fertile eggs and rent the necessary equipment. Make arrangements with a farm to take the chicks after you have finished hatching them. Chicken eggs take approximately 21 days to hatch. The day that you start, make a *"chick chain"* with the children. Each day let a child pull a chick off the chain. When the chain is short, you can begin to anticipate the chicks pecking out.

● Visit a local game farm. Enjoy the baby animals.

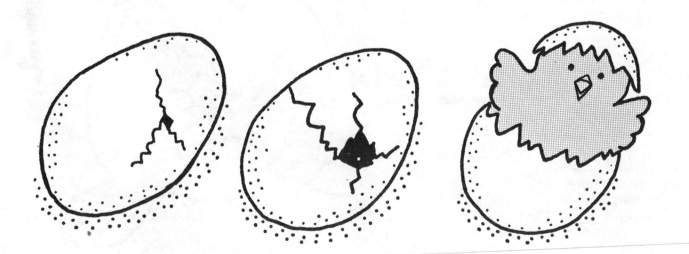

LANGUAGE GAMES

TALK ABOUT

Easter is a Christian holiday celebrating the resurrection of Jesus. Two days prior to the holiday, Jesus had been crucified. He died and was buried. On Easter Sunday, Christians believe that Jesus rose from the dead. Shortly after he rose, he began visiting his friends. They were very surprised and even afraid when they saw him, since they thought he had died. *"What do you think that Jesus and his friends talked about when they were together?"*

APRIL

LANGUAGE GAME

TRY TO REMEMBER
Have an Easter basket filled with all sorts of goodies. Talk about all of the things that are in the basket. After putting the goodies back, ask the children if they can remember what was in the basket. As they say an item, pull it out and put it on the floor for everyone to see. If there are several items left that the children are having difficulty remembering, give them clues.

EASTER BUNNY
What does the Easter Bunny have to do to prepare for Easter? Think about all of the items that go into an Easter basket, the requirements for his trip to all of the houses, what he will eat for energy, and so on.

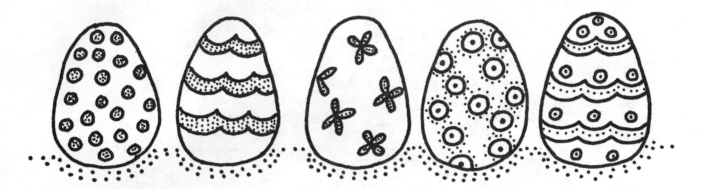

FELT BOARD FUN
• Make 5-10 different eggs out of felt for the teacher's Easter Basket. Make several matching sets of eggs for the children. Give each child a small basket with several felt eggs in it. Put one egg from your basket on the felt board. Have the children search their baskets for a matching egg. If they have one, let them come up to the felt board and put it near the first egg. Continue until all of the eggs are matched.

• Make a different chick for each child in the group. Make a duplicate set for the teacher. Give each child a chick. Now put one of the teacher's chicks on the felt board. Ask each child to look at his/hers and see if it matches the one that is on the board. If it does, have that child put the chick next to the one on the felt board. If it does not, have those children go *"Cheep-cheep-cheep!"* Put another chick on the board. Let one child match it and let the remaining children *"Cheep-cheep-cheep!"* Continue until all of the chicks have been matched. At the conclusion, have all of the children crouch down and waddle around the circle. Remember to *"Cheep-cheep-cheep!"*

CREATIVE THINKING
"The Easter Bunny has run out of eggs and other goodies to give the children. He still has five more families to visit and does not want to disappoint _____, _____, _____, _____, and _____.
(Name children in the class.) *What can the Easter Bunny leave for these children?"*

ACTIVE GAMES

HOPPING   At art, let each child make a headband with bunny ears and wear it to circle time. Move like a bunny:

Hop very quietly as if you are looking for vegetables.

Pretend you hear a strange noise and get scared. Hurry! Get away! Hop quickly in long strides.

Hop in short jumps.

EASTER
EGG ROLL
Pretend ping-pong balls are Easter eggs. Decorate each with non-toxic markers and give each child one. Beginning at a starting line, have them put the ball down and push it with their noses to a designated place. When they finish, give each child a badge to wear.
VARIATION:
Instead of pushing the *"egg"* with their noses, the children can blow it or move it along with their hand.

ACTIVE GAMES

TAPE THE TAIL ON THE BUNNY Make or buy a large Easter Bunny. Using fluffy cotton balls, let the children tape cotton onto the bunny tail. Depending on the age and/or abilities of the children, they can either cover their eyes or not.

MOVING Using a sturdy rope like a clothesline, form the shape of a giant jelly bean. Have the children sit around it. Talk about the colors of jelly beans. Decide what color this one is. Have the children stand and move around the jelly bean while singing this song to the tune of "*HERE WE GO 'ROUND THE MULBERRY BUSH.*"

> *We're sliding around the jelly bean,*
> *Jelly bean, jelly bean.*
> *We're sliding around the jelly bean,*
> *All day long.*
>
> *We're hopping around the jelly bean,*
>
> *We're walking . . .*
>
> *We're running . . .*
>
> *We're jumping . . .*

DUCK, DUCK RABBIT This is a variation of DUCK, DUCK, GOOSE. The children sit in a circle. One child walks around the circle tapping each child on the head while saying "*Duck*". When s/he comes to the child who will chase, she says "*Rabbit*". Then the first child tries to go around the circle and sit down in the empty space before the second child can catch him/her. During the chase, both children must hop like rabbits. Continue, letting other children enjoy the chase.

BOOKS

DU BOSE HEYWARD — *THE COUNTRY BUNNY AND THE GOLDEN SHOES*
MARGARET WISE BROWN — *RUNAWAY BUNNY*
ROBERT BRIGHT — *THE HOPPING BUNNY*
CHARLOTTE ZOLOTOW — *THE BUNNY WHO FOUND EASTER*
BEATRIX POTTER — *THE TALE OF PETER RABBIT*

ARBOR DAY

FOR OPENERS

READ THE BOOK A TREE IS NICE BY JANICE UDRY. DISCUSS ALL OF THE WAYS PEOPLE USE TREES. AFTER YOU HAVE DISCUSSED EACH WAY, ASK THE CHILDREN, "DID YOU EVER USE A TREE THAT WAY?" IF THEY DID, HAVE THEM ANSWER 'YES' BY SWAYING LIKE A TREE IN THE WIND. IF THEY DID NOT, HAVE THEM SIT STRAIGHT AND TALL, NOT MOVING AT ALL.

FINGERPLAYS

OAK TREE

Here is an oak tree, straight and tall
And here are its branches wide,
Here is a nest of twigs and moss,
With three little birds inside.

TREES

Elm trees stretch and stretch so wide.
Their limbs reach out on every side.
Pine trees stretch and stretch so high.
They nearly reach up to the sky.
Willows droop and droop so low,
Their branches sweep the ground below.

FIELD TRIPS

● If your town has an Arbor Day celebration, walk over to it and enjoy watching the townspeople plant a new tree, bush, or hedge. If not, take a walk to a nearby park, forest preserve, tree nursery, or nature center. Bring several magnifying glasses with you so that the children can closely examine the bark of the trees. Have them feel the bark. How does it feel? Look for short trees, tall trees, fat trees, and skinny ones. Are there any trees that would be good for climbing? Which ones and why? While you are looking at the trees, notice any animal homes in the trunks, on the limbs or near the tree.

CLASSROOM VISITOR

Invite a member of the Agricultural Extension Service to talk with the children about trees. Let him/her explain how trees grow, why they are cut down, and how the wood is used.

LANGUAGE GAMES

TALK ABOUT
Have books available about woods animals. Discuss the different animals that make their homes in trees. If you saw any animal homes on your field trip, discuss them in depth with the children.

CREATIVE THINKING
Have the children think of all of the things that they know that are made from wood. Make a list of the items as the children say them. After awhile, have them look around the room and see what things are made from wood.
EXTENSION:
Make a wood collage at art. Use wood products like spools, clothespins, pencils, sawdust, and so forth.

FELT BOARD FUN
Have a variety of green felt leaves. Put all of the leaves on the felt board. Talk about how each type of tree has a different leaf. Some leaves are small, some large, some have pointed edges, and some rounded.
EXTENSION:
Make several duplicate sets of the leaves. Put them on the floor so that everyone can see them. Sort the leaves. As you sort them, talk about why those particular leaves go together. After circle time, put the leaves on a special table for the children to continue sorting. They may create other ways to categorize.

ACTIVE GAMES

PLANT A TREE
Plant a seedling near the classroom. Let all of the children have an opportunity to help dig the hole. Once planted, let each child take a turn standing next to the tree and see how tall s/he is compared to the tree. Thoughout the rest of the Spring and Summer, the children should take turns caring for it. After several months, measure again.

BOOKS

JANICE UDRY — *A TREE IS NICE*
DONALD CARRICK — *THE TREE*
CLYDE ROBERT BULLA — *A TREE IS A PLANT*
SHEL SILVERSTEIN — *THE GIVING TREE*

MAY DAY

FOR OPENERS

DURING FREE PLAY, MAKE A MAYPOLE WITH THE CHILDREN. FASTEN LONG, COLORFUL STREAMERS TO A TREE OR POLE. HAVE ENOUGH STREAMERS FOR ALL OF THE CHILDREN AND ADULTS TO HAVE ONE FOR THE MAYPOLE DANCE. BEGIN THE CIRCLE TIME WITH SINGING AND DANCING. SING THE SONG SEVERAL TIMES BEFORE YOU BEGIN TO DANCE TO THE TUNE OF *"HERE WE GO 'ROUND THE MULBERRY BUSH"*:

HERE WE GO 'ROUND THE MAYPOLE, THE MAYPOLE, THE MAYPOLE.
HERE WE GO 'ROUND THE MAYPOLE, ALL ON A MAY DAY MORNING.

DANCING: HAVE EACH PERSON HOLD ONE OF THE STREAMERS. BEGIN SINGING THE SONG AND WALK AROUND THE MAYPOLE. WHEN YOU HAVE FINISHED SINGING THE SONG ONE TIME, REVERSE DIRECTION, WALK AGAIN AND SING THE SONG. CONTINUE THE GAME BY USING DIFFERENT MOVEMENTS AROUND THE MAYPOLE AS YOU SING.

FINGERPLAYS

FLOWER PLAY

If I were a little flower
Sleeping underneath the ground,
I'd raise my head and grow and grow,
And stretch my arms and grow and grow,
And nod my head and say:
"I'm glad to see you all today."

RELAXING FLOWERS

Five little flowers
Standing in the sun;
See their heads nodding,
Bowing, one by one.

Down, down, down
Falls the gentle rain
And the five little flowers
Lift up their heads again!

MY FLOWER BED

See the blue and yellow blossoms
In the flower bed.
The daisy spreads its petals wide
The tulip bows its head.

FIELD TRIPS

● Make May Baskets during art. At circle time, walk to a nearby hospital, retirement home, or orphanage. Bring the May Baskets to the people who live there. (Be certain to arrange this visit ahead of time.)

LANGUAGE GAMES

FLOWERS

Have a vase of several real flowers that have a strong smell. Let the children smell each flower. Do they have a favorite one? What do they like about their favorite flower — the smell, the color, the shape?

COLOR MATCH

Make a color wheel using the 8 basic colors. Paint several clothespins to match each color on the wheel. Have pictures of different flowers or real flowers. Hold up one flower. Talk about all of the colors in the flower. Have the children decide which color they see the most. Have a child get a clothespin which matches the predominant color of the flower and clip it onto the matching space on the color wheel.

BEE IN THE GARDEN

On a large piece of posterboard, draw a simple garden filled with colored flowers. Cut several slits in the different petals, in the leaves, on the ground, and in the sky. Make a bee out of posterboard which will fit into the slits you have made. The bee is looking for a flower with lots of pollen. She is going to fly from one flower to the next. As the bee is flying, have the children cover their eyes and make a *buzzing* sound. When the bee lands (Put her in a slit.) tell the children, *"Stop buzzing, open your eyes, and see if you can find where the bee has landed."* When they know, have them point to the place. Then have someone tell where the bee has landed. Continue the game by having the children close their eyes again, making a *buzzing* sound, and you put the bee into a different slit. Have the children open their eyes and find the bee again.

BOOKS

MARIANA — *MISS FLORA McFLIMSEY'S MAY DAY*

CINCO DE MAYO

FOR OPENERS

CINCO DE MAYO CELEBRATES AN IMPORTANT MEXICAN VICTORY OVER THE FRENCH SOLDIERS IN 1862. HAVE A MEXICAN FLAG AND A UNITED STATES FLAG. FIRST EXPLAIN THAT COUNTRIES HAVE DIFFERENT FLAGS. POINT TO THE UNITED STATES FLAG AND TELL THE CHILDREN THAT THIS IS THE FLAG OF THE UNITED STATES. PUT THE UNITED STATES FLAG AWAY. NOW DISCUSS THE MEXICAN FLAG. ASK THE CHILDREN "WHAT COLORS DO YOU SEE IN THE MEXICAN FLAG? WHICH WAY DO THE STRIPES GO, UP AND DOWN OR ACROSS?" COMPARE THE STRIPES TO THE UNITED STATES FLAG. HAVE THE CHILDREN LOOK CLOSELY AT THE COAT OF ARMS IN THE CENTER OF THE MEXICAN FLAG. CAN THEY RECOGNIZE WHAT THE PICTURE IS?

RECIPES

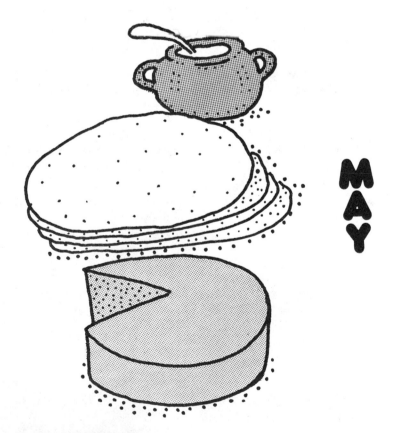

QUESADILLAS

YOU'LL NEED

1 Dozen Flour Tortillas
1 lb. Cheese - either
    Cheddar or Monterey Jack, grated or
    sliced thin
½ c. sugar (optional)

TO MAKE: Warm tortillas on a griddle or grill to soften. Place cheese on half of the tortilla and fold over and return to grill. Let it toast a little on one side, then turn over to toast the other side long enough to melt the cheese. When cheese is melted remove from grill and cut into halves or fourths to serve. Quesadillas may be sprinkled with a little sugar if a sweet taste is desired.

CLASSROOM VISITOR

Ask a family who has been in Mexico during Cinco de Mayo to visit the center and talk about the Cinco de Mayo parades.

LANGUAGE GAMES

SPEAKING
SPANISH

Learn to count to ten in Spanish.
1 — Uno
2 — Dos
3 — Tres
4 — Cuatro
5 — Cinco
6 — Seis
7 — Siete
8 — Ocho
9 — Nueve
10 — Diez

INSTRUMENTS

Have a guitar and maracas. Let the children strum the guitar and shake the maracas. Then play Mexican music. Have the children listen carefully to it. Let them identify when they hear the guitar and the maracas. When they hear the guitar, have them pretend to strum. When they hear the maracas, have them shake their arms.

PARADES

Parades are part of the Cinco de Mayo celebrations. Have the children cover their eyes. Play some parade music. Ask them to think about parades. After several minutes, stop the music. Ask the children what they saw in their minds.

ACTIVE GAMES

PINATAS

Several days before Cinco de Mayo, have the children enjoy making a paper mache pinata. On Cinco de Mayo, hang the pinata and have the fun of breaking it open. Have the children stand in a wide circle. Each child should get a chance to hit the pinata with a stick such as a broom handle. As the children are watching, have them clap in rhythm.

BOOKS

JUNE BEHRENS — *FIESTA*

MOTHER'S DAY

FOR OPENERS

MOTHER'S DAY IS A TIME TO THINK ABOUT ALL OF THE SPECIAL WOMEN IN THE CHILDREN'S LIVES. HAVE THE CHILDREN NAME SEVERAL WOMEN THAT ARE IMPORTANT TO THEM AND WHY THEY ARE SPECIAL. AS THE CHILDREN ARE TALKING, MAKE A LIST OF ALL THE REASONS THAT WOMEN ARE SPECIAL. NOW GO BACK TO THE FIRST REASON ON THE LIST. POINT TO THE WORD OR PICTURE AND SAY TO THE CHILDREN, "LOVE IS THE FIRST THING ON THE LIST. IF YOU KNOW A WOMAN WHO GIVES YOU LOVE, STAND UP. THE SECOND WORD ON THE LIST IS FOOD. IF YOU KNOW A WOMAN WHO GIVES YOU FOOD, JUMP UP AND DOWN." CONTINUE THROUGH THE LIST OF WORDS IN THIS MANNER.

EXTENSION: AFTER CIRCLE TIME, LET EACH CHILD MAKE A BIG FLOWER FOR ONE OF THE SPECIAL WOMEN IN HIS/HER LIFE. WHEN EACH CHILD IS FINISHED, HAVE HIM/HER TELL YOU WHICH WORD TO WRITE IN THE MIDDLE OF THE FLOWER. WRITE IT FOR THE CHILD. HAVE THE CHILD TAKE THE FLOWER HOME AND GIVE IT TO THAT WOMAN.

FINGERPLAYS

STARS

At night I see the twinkling stars
And a great big smiling moon.
My Mommy tucks me into bed
And sings a good-night tune.

EVENING CHORES

The dishes need washing,
Mother and I are a team.
She washes, I wipe them
Until they all gleam.

Dad and sister are helping.
They're sweeping the floors.
We all work together,
When doing the chores.
　　　　Dick Wilmes

RECIPES

FACES

YOU'LL NEED

Crackers
Spreadable cheese or peanut butter
Small pieces of vegetables

TO MAKE: Have the children sit around the ingredients. Let them spread cheese or peanut butter on their crackers. Then using the vegetable bits, have them make an "X" or heart symbolizing love for their mothers.

LANGUAGE GAMES

TALK ABOUT

Discuss different things about mothers. Ask the children, *"Who has a mother that works away from home? What does your mother do when she goes to work? What jobs does your mother do at home? What does your mother do for fun?"*

DESCRIBING YOUR MOTHER

If possible, have the children bring in a picture of their mothers. Talk about what mothers look like. Ask questions like, *"What color hair does your mother have? Color of eyes? Long hair or short hair? What does she like to wear?*

CREATIVE THINKING

Ask the children, *"If you could give your mother any present, what would you give her?"*

ACTIVE GAMES

MOTHER SAYS

Play *MOTHER SAYS* — (a variation of Simon Says) using the activities that the children described in TALK ABOUT. For example, *"Mother says, make the bed.* (The children pretend to make the bed.) *Mother says, set the table."* (The children do that.) When you simply give the command, such as *"Mow the grass"*, children who obey the command are usually out. In *MOTHER SAYS*, these children simply keep on playing.

BOOKS

JUDITH VIORST — *MY MAMA SAYS THERE AREN'T ANY ZOMBIES, GHOSTS, VAMPIRES, CREATURES, DEMONS, MONSTERS, FIENDS, GOBLINS, OR THINGS*
MARIA POLUSHKIN — *MOTHER, MOTHER, I WANT ANOTHER*
MARJORIE FLACK — *ASK MR. BEAR*

MEMORIAL DAY

FOR OPENERS

HAVE THE CHILDREN WEAR A SMOCK TO CIRCLE TIME. HAVE A UNITED STATES FLAG FOR THEM TO SEE. TALK ABOUT THE RED, WHITE, AND BLUE COLORS IN THE FLAG. AFTER YOU HAVE TALKED ABOUT THE COLORS FOR SEVERAL MINUTES, BRING OUT A WHITE SHEET. HAVE THE CHILDREN SIT AROUND THE SHEET AND SPONGE PAINT WITH RED AND BLUE COLORS. AFTER IT IS DRY, HANG IT ON A LARGE WALL. KEEP IT HANGING UNTIL AFTER THE FOURTH OFJULY. (IF THE CHILDREN ARE OLDER AND CAN MAKE THE DESIGN OF THE FLAG, THEN HELP THEM SPONGE PAINT IN A MORE ORGANIZED FASHION.)

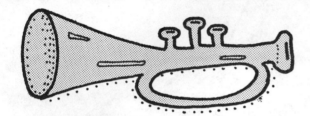

FINGERPLAYS

TEN LITTLE FINGER SOLDIERS

Ten little finger soldiers
Standing in a row.
Up the hill - down the hill,
Marching they will go.
When they're up, they're high.
When they're down - they're low.
Ten little finger soldiers
Marching in a row.

DRUMS

Boom! Boom! Boom!
Goes the big brass drum.
Rat-a-tat-tat goes the little one.
And down the street in line we come
To the boom, boom, boom
Of the big brass drum
And the rat-a-tat-tat
Of the little one.

THE FINGER BAND

The Finger Band is coming to town,
Coming to town, coming to town
The Finger Band is coming to town,
So early in the morning.

This is the way they wear their hats,
Wear their hats, wear their hats.
This is the way they wear their hats,
So early in the morning.

This is the way they wave their flags,

This is the way they beat their drums,

This is the way they blow their horns,

The Finger Band is going away,
Going away, going away.
The Finger Band is going away,
So early in the morning.

RECIPES

RED, WHITE, AND BLUE SALAD

YOU'LL NEED
Strawberries
Blueberries
Bananas

TO MAKE: Clean and fix the fruit. Put in a bowl and mix gently. Have the fruit snack outside. Pretend you are on a picnic and sit on a big picnic blanket.

CLASSROOM VISITOR

Ask several students who are in the high school marching band to visit the class. Have them wear their uniforms and bring their instruments. Have them play some marches and let the children march to their music.

LANGUAGE GAMES

TRY TO REMEMBER

Many families go on picnics to celebrate Memorial Day. Make a list with the children of all the things that they will need to bring on the picnic. The next day, sit on a blanket and have all of the items they listed in a big picnic basket. See if they can remember some of the things from the previous day. As the children remember each thing, take it out of the basket and put it on the blanket.

PARADES

Talk about parades. Ask the children if they have ever been to a parade with their family. Ask them who they saw in the parades. If they have difficulty remembering, give them clues. What do the people in the parade do?

ACTIVE GAMES

PICNIC GAMES

People play lots of group games at picnics. Go outside with the children and enjoy several games. Remember, everyone *wins!*
- Any type of tag.
- Races — Run, hop, skip.
- Follow the leader.

BOOKS

ED EMBERLEY —*PARADE BOOK*

FLAG DAY

FOR OPENERS

BETSY ROSS MADE ONE OF THE FIRST AMERICAN FLAGS OVER 200 YEARS AGO. IT HAD 13 RED AND WHITE STRIPES AND 13 STARS IN THE SHAPE OF A CIRCLE ON IT. THE AMERICAN FLAG HAS CHANGED MANY TIMES SINCE THEN. TODAY THE FLAG HAS 13 STRIPES AND 50 STARS.

AS EACH CHILD COMES TO CIRCLE TIME, GIVE HIM/HER A WHITE STAR. HAVE THE CHILDREN SIT IN A CIRCLE AND HOLD THEIR STAR. WHEN ALL OF THE CHILDREN ARE THERE, GO AROUND THE CIRCLE COUNTING OFF TO 13. HAVE EACH CHILD STAND UP AS S/HE SAYS HIS/HER NUMBER.

EXTENSION: HAVE THE CHILDREN SAVE THEIR STARS FOR ART. HAVE THEM COLLAGE THE STARS WITH RED AND BLUE TEXTURES.

FINGERPLAYS

OUR FLAG

The flag is coming. We see it now,
It's red and blue and white.
With stars and stripes, it's held so high.
It's such a wonderful sight.

We are proud to hold our faces up
And stand so straight and tall,
To place our hands upon our hearts
And pray for peace for all.
Dick Wilmes

RECIPES

POPSICLES

YOU'LL NEED

Pineapple juice
Grape juice
Cranberry juice

Popsicle sticks
Small paper cups

TO MAKE: Fill the paper cups ¾ full of juice. Put the cups in the freezer. When the juice begins to freeze, put a popsicle stick in the middle of each cup. When frozen, peel the cup away and serve red, white and blue treats.

LANGUAGE GAMES

TALK ABOUT   As the children go home on June 13th, tell them to look for flags on their way to school the next day. On Flag Day, have the children name all of the places where they saw flags. If any of them have a flag at home, talk about where the flag is hanging.

FELT BOARD FUN   Make between five and seven pairs of different sized white stars. Mix up the stars and put them on the felt board. Have the children look at all of the stars and find pairs that are the same size.

THE FLAG   Have a United States flag for the children to look at.

- Have the children count the red stripes and then the white stripes. Count the stars in one of the rows. Count the rows.
- Point to a red stripe. Have all of the children wearing red stand up and point to the red in their clothes.
- Point to a white stripe. Have everyone wearing white stand up and tell what s/he is wearing that is white.
- Point to the field of blue. Have everyone wearing blue stand up. Have the sitting children look at those who are standing and tell what is blue.
- Have the children stand who are not wearing red, white, or blue. Have these children tell one color that they are wearing.

JUNE

ACTIVE GAMES

MARCHING   Using red, white and blue streamers, march to patriotic or marching music. If it is a nice day, march around the block waving the flags or streamers.

BOOKS

PETER SPIER — *STAR SPANGLED BANNER*

FATHER'S DAY

FOR OPENERS

FATHER'S DAY IS A TIME TO REMEMBER THE SPECIAL MEN IN CHILDREN'S LIVES. HAVE THE CHILDREN TELL WHO IS SPECIAL TO THEM AND WHY. AFTER SEVERAL CHILDREN HAVE SAID WHO IS SPECIAL AND HAVE GIVEN THEIR REASONS, PLAY A MEMORY GAME. HAVE THE CHILDREN WHO HAVE TALKED, STAND UP. ASK THE CHILDREN "WHO CAN REMEMBER WHICH MAN IS SPECIAL TO AMY? (ANSWER) CAN ANYONE REMEMBER WHY HER UNCLE IS SPECIAL TO HER?" (ANSWER) ASK THE SAME QUESTION ABOUT THE OTHER CHILDREN WHO ARE STANDING. IF NOBODY CAN REMEMBER, HAVE THE CHILD REPEAT WHO IS SPECIAL AND WHY. HAVE THOSE CHILDREN SIT DOWN AND LET SEVERAL MORE TALK ABOUT MEN IN THEIR LIVES. ONCE AGAIN AFTER SEVERAL HAVE TALKED, PLAY THE MEMORY GAME. DO THIS UNTIL ALL OF THE CHILDREN HAVE HAD AN OPPORTUNITY TO TALK.

FINGERPLAYS

BABY'S NAP

This is a baby ready for a nap.
Lay him down in his father's lap.
Cover him up so he won't peep.
Rock him 'til he's fast asleep.

HELPING MY DAD

I like to help my dad a lot
To rake the lawn or dry a pot.
It doesn't matter what's to be done.
When we do it together,
It's always more fun!!
Dick Wilmes

L^NGUAGE GA^ES

TALK ABOUT
Have pictures of men doing all types of activities — reading, working, playing, sleeping, etc. Hold up one picture at a time. Have the children look at it. Talk briefly about what the man is doing. If the children know a man who does this, have them stand up. Those who are standing can tell the other children who they know who does that particular activity. Continue until you have discussed all of the pictures.

TRY TO REMEMBER
Have the children think about all of the men with whom they have fun. Those who want can talk into a tape recorder about the fun they have had. When everyone has had a chance to talk, rewind the tape. All of those who talked into the tape recorder should stand. Play the tape back. See if the person who talked can recognize his/her own voice. When the person hears his/her voice, have him/her sit down.

FELT BOARD FUN
Make a large silhouette of a blank face and several different eyes, noses, hair styles, beards, mustaches, etc. Have fun making different faces. Talk about the different features. Have the children notice features that are the same as those of men who they know. Can any of the children make faces that look like someone they know? After circle time, put the felt board and pieces on a table where the children can continue to make faces of men they know.

JUNE

111

ACTIVE GAMES

SINGING

Make a list of the activities that men do around the house. Read the list when finished. Now stand up, sing, and do the actions of the activities you have just talked about. Sing the song to the tune of "HERE WE GO 'ROUND THE MULBERRY BUSH"

This is the way we vacuum the rug,
Vacuum the rug, vacuum the rug.
This is the way we vacuum the rug,
All on a Monday morning.

This is the way we fix the dinner,

Continue the song using the activities that the children have created.

BOOKS

FRANK ASCH —*JUST LIKE DADDY*
MIRIAM STECHER —*DADDY AND BEN TOGETHER*

first day of SUMMER

FOR OPENERS

HAVE LARGE PICTURES OF DIFFERENT MODES OF TRANSPORTATION. ASK THE CHILDREN IF THEIR FAMILY IS GOING ON A SUMMER VACATION. WHERE? HOW WILL THEY TRAVEL? PASS OUT ALL OF THE TRANSPORTATION PICTURES. STAND BEHIND THE FIRST CHILD HOLDING A PICTURE AND ASK, "WHO IS GOING TO TRAVEL IN A 'TRAIN'?" LET THOSE CHILDREN STAND UP AND MAKE A SOUND LIKE A TRAIN WHISTLE. GO TO THE NEXT CHILD AND ASK, "WHO IS GOING BY 'CAR'?" THESE CHILDREN WILL STAND UP AND MAKE A SOUND LIKE A CAR HORN. CONTINUE UNTIL YOU HAVE TALKED ABOUT ALL OF THE FORMS OF TRANSPORTATION.

FINGERPLAYS

I DIG, DIG, DIG

I dig, dig, dig,
And I plant some seeds.
I rake, rake, rake,
And I pull some weeds.

I wait and watch
And soon I know
My garden sprouts
And starts to grow.

A LITTLE BOY'S WALK

A little boy went walking
One lovely summer day.
He saw a little rabbit
That quickly ran away.

He saw a shining river
Go winding in and out,
And little fishes in it
Were swimming all about.

(Repeat for Little Girl's Walk)

DAY AT THE BEACH

Ocean breeze blowing,
Feet kick and splash,
Ocean waves breaking,
On rocks with a crash.

Boys finding seashells,
Girls sifting sand,
Friends building castles
As high as they can.

I stretch my arms out
Far as they'll reach
Oh, my what fun
On this day at the beach.

BEEHIVE

Here is the little beehive.
Where are the bees?
Hidden away where nobody sees.
Soon they come creeping out of the hive.
One, two, three, four, five.

JUNE

RECIPES

<u>OLD FASHIONED LEMONADE</u>
(serves 4 to 5)

YOU'LL NEED

2 lemons
3 to 4 T. honey
3½ to 4 cups water
ice cubes.

TO MAKE: Cut the lemons in half and squeeze out the juice. Dissolve the honey into the lemon juice. Add water and grated lemon peels. Let set for 10 minutes or more to improve the flavor. Serve over plenty of ice.

from COME AND GET IT
by Kathleen Baxter

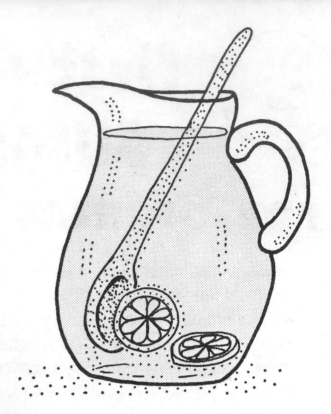

FIELD TRIPS

● Take an early morning walk. Look and listen for the signs of Summer. When you return, take out the Seasonal Chart. Talk about the signs of all of the other seasons. Now add Summer. Ask the children what they saw and heard on the walk that made them think of Summer. List what the children say. Hang up the chart so that the children can see all four seasons.

LANGUAGE GAMES

TRY TO
REMEMBER

Discuss what they will take with them on their vacation trip. Have an empty suitcase and let the children pretend that they are packing. What would they put in the suitcase? Once they have named 4 or 5 items, go back and review them. *"First you put in _____. Next you put in _____."* Continue until they have remembered everything. Go ahead and name more items for the suitcase and review again.

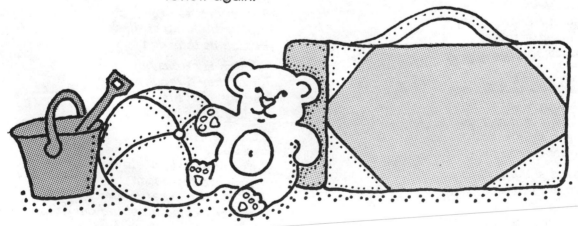

LANGUAGE GAMES

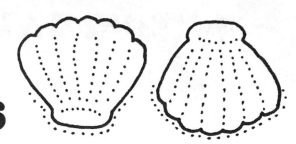

**EXPORING
SHELLS**

Have several each of 5 or 6 different types of shells. Mix them up and lay them on the floor for all of the children to see. Pick up one shell. Ask the children to find the shells that match the one that you are holding. Put them in a group off to the side. Pick up another shell and find the matching ones. Continue until all of the shells are matched.

EXTENSION:

Mix up the shells again. Have the children come up and pick one they would like to look at more closely. Have them go back to their places and sit down. Ask the children to decide what colors are in their shell, if it smells, what shape it is, if there is a special design in the shell, any points, and so on. Have several magnifying glasses for the children to use while examining the shells.

FELT BOARD FUN

Have a large felt boy and girl. Make different Summer clothes that children wear - shorts, bathing suits, swimming caps, strap top blouses and flip-flops. Put all of the Summer clothes on the felt board. Then add some Fall and Winter clothers - boots, snowsuit, sweater, hat, and others. Ask the children which clothes they wear in the Summer. Have several children tell you. Now ask when they wear the other clothes. Take away the inappropriate clothes as you talk about them. All of the Summer clothes are left. Point to one piece of clothing and ask, *"When do you wear a bathing suit?"* Let the children talk about their swimming experiences. Go onto another article of clothing and discuss. Continue.

**CREATIVE
MOVEMENT**

Make a bright yellow sun out of a paper plate. Glue the plate to a paint stick. Hold up the sun. Talk about how hot the sun is during the Summer. Ask the children *"How can we keep cool when Mr. (Ms.) Sun is making us so hot?"* Make a list of their suggestions in words or pictures. Post for all to enjoy.

JUNE

ACTIVE GAMES

BUGS, BUGS

There are lots of bugs around during the Summer. Have the children name some that they know. Ask how they sound. Let the children make the noise. Talk about how the bugs move. Have them imitate the movement.

EXTENSION:

The following day, set-up a maze outside, using the equipment, tires, ropes, and the landscape itself. First let the children go normally through the maze. Next let them pretend to be a bug and make bug noises as they go through the maze.

CREATIVE THINKING

Let the children name things that they do at the beach. Now pretend to go to the beach for a trip. *"Oh, it is a very warm day. Let's go to the beach to cool off. Quickly, we'll make a picnic lunch.* (Let the children pretend to make a lunch.) *Put the lunch, pails, balls, and kite into the car. Now we're ready. Let's get going.* (Have the children pretend that they are driving to the beach. Talk about what they see on the way.) *Good, we're at the beach. Everyone help carry our things. Let's walk down to the shore.* (Have the children walk around the circle carrying something. Stop when they get back to their place.) *Let's go swimming first.* (Pretend to swim.) *Oh, the water feels so good. Here comes a wave. Swish. Let's go play catch.* (Have several small balls or bean bags and let the children play catch.) *It's fun to fly kites on the beach, too. There are no trees for the kites to get caught in.* (Give each child a scarf or streamer. Let him/her move around the room flying his kite.) *Children, it's time for lunch.* (Have them come back, sit down and pretend to eat. Talk about what you are eating. After lunch, continue by adding other movements that the children talked about in the beginning discussion.) *We are all very tired. Time to go home. I'll drive while all of you curl up and take a rest."* (Have children lie in place. You drive home. Maybe sing a lullabye.)

BOOKS

JANICE MAY UDRY — *MARY ANN'S MUD DAY*
LEO LIONNI — *SWIMMY*
LEO LIONNI — *THE BIGGEST HOUSE IN THE WORLD*
EZRA JACK KEATS — *OVER IN THE MEADOW*
AILEEN FISHER — *ONCE WE WENT ON A PICNIC*
VIRGINIA POULET — *BLUE BUGS VEGETABLE GARDEN*
ALVIN TRESSELT — *I SAW THE SEA COME IN*
ELEANOR SCHICK — *A CITY IN THE SUMMER*

FOURTH of JULY

FOR OPENERS

THE FOURTH OF JULY COMMEMORATES THE SIGNING OF THE DECLARATION OF INDEPENDENCE OF THE UNITED STATES FROM ENGLAND. EVERY JULY 4TH, THE PEOPLE OF THE UNITED STATES CELEBRATE FREEDOM BY WATCHING COLORFUL FIREWORKS, ENJOYING FAMILY AND NEIGHBORHOOD PICNICS, AND/OR VENTURING AWAY FOR LONG WEEK-ENDS. THE STREETS AND HOUSES ARE FILLED WITH UNITED STATES FLAGS. ALMOST EVERY TOWN ACROSS THE COUNTRY HAS A PARADE WITH BANDS, VEHICLES, CLOWNS, AND FLOATS.

DISCUSS PARADES WITH THE CHILDREN. ALTHOUGH PARADES ARE FUN, THEY ARE NOISY. DISCUSS THE NOISE THAT THE FIRE ENGINES, POLICE CARS AND AMBULANCES MAKE. HAVE THE CHILDREN MAKE THE NOISES WITH THEIR MOUTHS. WHO MAKES A LOUDER NOISE, THE CHILDREN OR THE EMERGENCY VEHICLES? TALK ABOUT THE NOISE THAT BANDS MAKE. HAVE THE CHILDREN PRETEND THAT THEY ARE TOOTING HORNS, BEATING DRUMS, AND BANGING CYMBALS. WHO IS LOUDER, THE REAL BAND OR THE CHILDREN? THERE ARE MANY OTHER SOUNDS IN A PARADE. SEE HOW MANY THE CHILDREN CAN THINK OF. IF THEY NEED CLUES, HELP THEM THINK OF CARS HONKING THEIR HORNS, TRICK RIDERS MANUEVERING THEIR MOTORCYCLES, AND SOLDIERS FIRING RIFLES AND CANNONS.

JULY

FINGERPLAYS

LET'S PRETEND

Let's pretend we're having fun
At a picnic everyone.
Then some picnic pets come 'round.
Birds that flutter to the ground.
Crickets who can jump so funny,
And a wiggly little bunny.
Butterflies on lazy wings,
Squirrels, and lots of other things!
Let's pretend that we are all
Picnic pets who've come to call.

FINGERPLAYS

WOODEN SOLDIERS

Wooden soldiers, red and blue,
Tramp, tramp, tramp, we march for you.
Wooden soldiers, here we come.
Boom, boom, boom, we beat the drum.

THE BAND

Listen to the band parade.
Little snare drums swell and fade.
Rat-a-tat-tat, rat-a-tat-tat,
Rat-a-tat-tat, tat, tat.

Down the street the marchers come.
I can hear the big old drum.
Br-r-r-rum, b-r-r-rum,
Br-r-rum-tum-tum.

Flutes are playing shrill and high,
As the players go marching by.
Deedle-dee, deedle-dee,
Deedle-dee-dee.

The big bassoons rumble and roar,
Deep bass notes out of them pour.
Rumble-rum, rumble-rum,
Rumble-rum-rum.

I can hear the trumpets, too,
Sounding clear and loud and true.
Toot-a-toot-too, toot-a-toot-too,
Toot-a-toot-too-too-too.

Slide trombones sound loud and sweet,
As the band marches down the street.
Tra-dum, tra-dum, tra-tra-tra,
Tra-dum, tra-dum, dum, dum.

LANGUAGE GAMES

TALK ABOUT

With all of the activity of the Fourth of July, talk with the children about safety, especially around fireworks. Once you have emphasized the safety rules, begin to discuss the brilliant colors of the fireworks. Have a long sheet of butcher paper, tempera paint, and brushes ready. Let the children enjoy painting fireworks in the sky. Hang up.

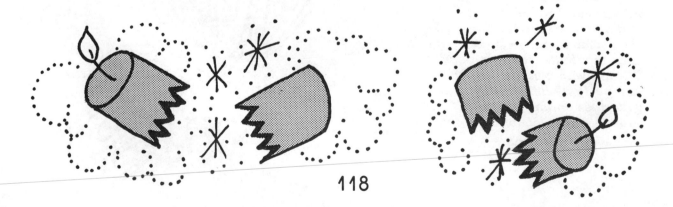

118

LA GUAGE GA ES

EXPLORING WATERMELON

Watermelon is a picnic favorite. Have a whole watermelon. Talk about the color of the outside which is called the rind. Next cut the watermelon into pieces. Give each child a piece to look at. Examine it carefully. *"What color is the inside? Are there seeds inside? Do we eat the seeds? What can we do with them?"*

EXTENSION:

Have the children remove all of the seeds from their piece of watermelon. Collect all of the seeds. After circle time, wash the seeds. When dry, collage them onto pink paper.

ACTIVE GAMES

PARADE

Several days before the holiday, decorate bikes, wagons, scooters, and other riding toys. When all of the vehicles are trimmed with streamers and other decorations, have a parade around the neighborhood.

BOOKS

GENE ZION — *THE SUMMER SNOWMAN*
RICHARD SCHACKBURG — *YANKEE DOODLE*

119

MOON DAY

MOON DAY COMMEMORATES THE LANDING OF THE FIRST UNITED STATES ASTRONAUTS ON THE MOON. MAKE A SIMPLE SPACESHIP OUT OF A PAPER TOWEL ROLL AND EXPLAIN TO THE CHILDREN HOW A SPACESHIP WORKS. AS THE SPACESHIP IS BLASTED OFF, THE BOOSTER ROCKETS ARE IGNITED. EACH SET OF ROCKETS BURNS UNTIL IT IS OUT OF FUEL AND THEN FALLS OFF. FINALLY THERE REMAINS ONLY THE SPACESHIP, WHICH CONTAINS THE COMMAND MODULE AND THE LUNAR LANDER. WHEN IT IS TIME TO LAND ON THE MOON, THE TWO ASTRONAUTS BOARD THE LUNAR LANDER AND TRAVEL TO THE SURFACE OF THE MOON. ONE ASTRONAUT STAYS IN THE COMMAND MODULE. AFTER THE TWO ASTRONAUTS HAVE COMPLETED THEIR WORK ON THE MOON, THEY RETURN TO THE COMMAND MODULE AND BEGIN THEIR TRIP BACK TO THE EARTH IN THE SPACESHIP.

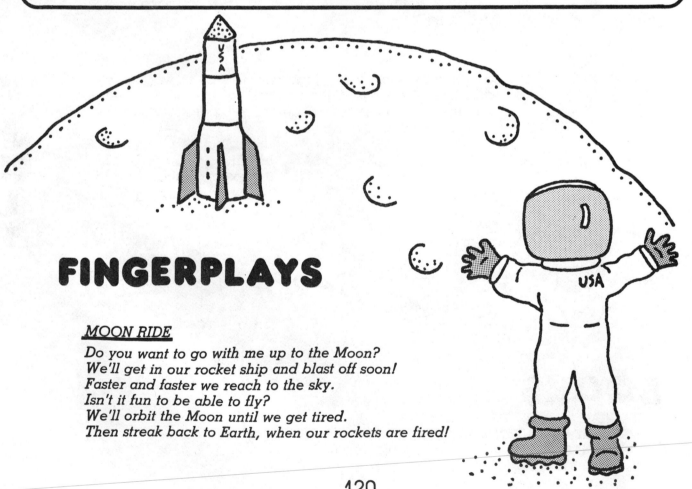

FINGERPLAYS

MOON RIDE

Do you want to go with me up to the Moon?
We'll get in our rocket ship and blast off soon!
Faster and faster we reach to the sky.
Isn't it fun to be able to fly?
We'll orbit the Moon until we get tired.
Then streak back to Earth, when our rockets are fired!

LA GUAGE GAMES

MOON TALK — Make space helmets out of five gallon ice cream cartons, which you can obtain from an ice cream store. Have the children bring the helmet to circle time. Introduce the children to a few *"space words"*. *"On the earth where we live we have gravity which pulls us to the ground. The Moon does not have as much gravity and therefore does not pull our bodies down as hard. When people move on the Moon, they almost float.* (Have the children pretend that they are on the Moon. How would they move? Let them move around the room as if they were exploring the Moon.) *Another fact about the Moon is that the air is lighter. When people are on the Moon, they need to wear space suits that have a special container with extra air which they need to breath.* (Have the children put on their space helmets and once again let them *"move around on the Moon."* This time breathing their extra air.)

CREATIVE THINKING — *"Pretend that you are an astronaut standing on the Moon. Look around. What do you see?*

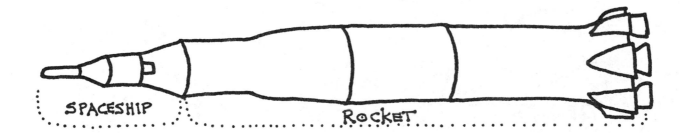

SPACESHIP .... ROCKET ....

ACTIVE GAMES

COUNT DOWN — Have the children sit in *"take-off"* position. Begin the *"count-down. Ten, nine, eight, seven, six, five, four, three, two, one — BLAST OFF."* When you reach *blast off*, have the children shoot up into the air. Do this several times.

MOON WALK — During the free play period before circle time, trace and then cut out patterns of the children's feet. Tape them all to the floor in a Moon Walk pattern. Remember to spread the feet far enough apart so that the children leap from one step to the next. During circle time, take a Moon Walk. Be certain to look around. *"What do you see? Be careful, there are gigantic holes in the Moon which are called craters."*

BOOKS

JANIS KNUDSEN WHEAT — *LET'S GO TO THE MOON*
GAIL HALEY — *JACK JOUETT'S RIDE*
EZRA JACK KEATS — *REGARDS TO THE MAN IN THE MOON*
FRANKLIN BRANLEY — *WHAT THE MOON IS LIKE*
FRANKLIN BRANLEY — *OXYGEN KEEPS YOU ALIVE*

JULY

BIRTHDAYS

FOR OPENERS

WHEN THE GROUP HAS GATHERED, SING "HAPPY BIRTHDAY" TO THE CHILD WHO IS CELEBRATING HIS/HER BIRTHDAY. LET THE BIRTHDAY CHILD STAY STANDING WHILE EVERYONE SINGS TO HIM/HER. WHEN FINISHED WITH THE SONG, EVERYONE CLAP FOR THE "SPECIAL" CHILD. ASK THE CHILD HOW OLD S/HE IS TODAY. WHATEVER THE AGE, HAVE THE GROUP COUNT TO THE AGE OF THE CHILD. AS THEY COUNT, HAVE THEM PUT UP FINGERS TO COINCIDE WITH THEIR COUNTING.

FINGERPLAYS

A BIRTHDAY

Today is _____'s birthday.
Let's make him (her) a cake.
Mix and stir, stir and mix,
Then into the oven to bake.

Here's our cake so nice and round.
We frost it pink and white.
We put four candles on it,
To make a birthday light.

FIVE BROWN PENNIES

Five brown pennies in my purse;
This one's for some gum;
This one's for a lollipop;
This one's for a drum.
These I'll save inside my purse,
Until your birthday comes.

BIRTHDAY CANDLES

Today I have a birthday.
I'm four years old, you see.
And here I have a birthday cake
Which you may share with me.
First we count the candles,
Count them, every one.
One, two, three, four,
The counting now is done.
Let's blow out the candles.
Out each flame will go.
"Wh. . ., wh. . ., wh. . ., wh. . .,"
As one by one we blow.

WHAT AM I BAKING?

Sift the flour and break an egg.
Add some salt and a bit of nutmeg.
A spoon of butter, a cup of milk,
Stir and beat as fine as silk.
Want to know what I'm going to bake?
Sh-sh, it's a secret!
A BIRTHDAY CAKE!!!

RECIPES

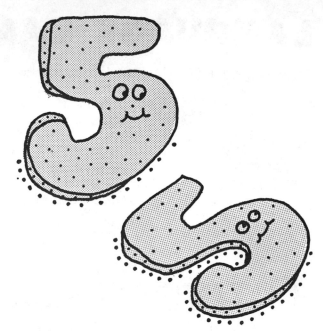

SUGAR COOKIES

YOU'LL NEED

Your favorite sugar cookie recipe
Number cookie cutters

TO MAKE: Make your favorite sugar cookie recipe. Using number cookie cutters, cut the dough into the age of the birthday child. Bake as instructed. Serve at snack.

LANGUAGE GAMES

BIRTHDAY HAT — Make a hat that the birthday child can wear during circle time. The hat should have a slit in it so that the number can be changed depending on the age of the child. Before the child puts the hat on, have everyone look at the number. Say the number and then let the group repeat it.

TALK ABOUT — Let the child tell how s/he will celebrate his/her birthday at home. If the child is hesitant, help him/her along by asking leading questions such as *"Do you think that you will have a birthday cake?"* Ask the child how s/he likes being a new age. Does it feel different than yesterday? How? Let other children answer this question also.

FELT BOARD FUN   Make a large birthday cake without any candles on it. Make separate birthday candles. Put five or six birthday candles on the felt board next to the cake. Let the birthday child put the appropriate number of candles on the cake. When s/he has done it, have everyone count the candles.

CREATIVE THINKING   *"You are having a birthday party with your friends. Your dad goes into the kitchen to get your birthday cake. It is gone. What could have happened to your cake? What can you do now?*

ACTIVE GAMES

BALLOON PLAY   Blow up several balloons. Let the children try to keep them up in the air. When they land on the ground, simply toss them up again.
VARIATION:
Bend coat hangers into diamond shapes. Tape the handles for safety. Pull nylon stockings over the diamond shapes to form swatters. Let each child have a swatter. Now have the children keep the balloons up in the air by hitting them with swatters.

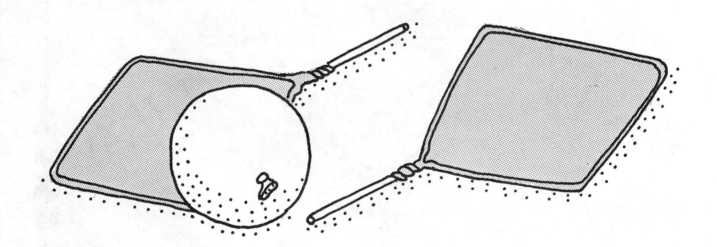

BOOKS

CHARLOTTE ZOLOTOW — *OVER AND OVER*
ERIC CARLE — *THE SECRET BIRTHDAY MESSAGE*
EZRA JACK KEATS — *A LETTER TO AMY*
PAT HUTCHINS — *HAPPY BIRTHDAY SAM*

LOCAL
HOLIDAYS

Your Reactions, Please

We are happy that you have selected to use THE CIRCLE TIME BOOK. We hope that you find its contents both refreshing and helpful as you plan activities to do with your children each year. Would you please share your reactions to help us as we prepare future publications.

1. Which type of activities did you find the most useful for your needs? Please rank in order of preference from 1 to 7, 1 being the most helpful.

    For Openers_____

    Fingerplays _____

    Field Trips _____

    Recipes_____

    Classroom Visitor _____

    Language Games_____

    Active Games_____

2. Is there a type of activity which we should include in our upcoming publication, THE EVERYDAY CIRCLE TIME BOOK?

    Yes _____

    No _____

    If YES, please specify. What type of activity should it be?

3. Would patterns for the felt board activities be helpful?

    Yes _____

    No_____

4. Tell us some of your favorite things about THE CIRCLE TIME BOOK.

5. Do you have any other comments about THE CIRCLE TIME BOOK which you wish to share with us?

Thank you for your comments. Please clip out, fold in thirds, staple and drop into the mail. We'll pay the postage (that's only fair).

Clip Here

Watch for the forthcoming BUILDING BLOCKS Publication
THE EVERYDAY CIRCLE TIME BOOK

If you would like notification of our new books and/or a sample of BUILDING BLOCKS Newspaper, fill out the coupon below.

_____ BUILDING BLOCKS NEWSPAPER   _____ Forthcoming Books

Name _____

Address _____

City _____

State _____ Zip _____

- - - - - - - - - - - - - Fold Here First - - - - - - - - - - - - -

Staple

BUSINESS REPLY CARD

FIRST CLASS PERMIT NO.31   DUNDEE ILLINOIS

POSTAGE WILL BE PAID BY ADDRESSEE

BUILDING BLOCKS

BOX 31

DUNDEE ILLINOIS   60118

NO POSTAGE
NECESSARY
IF MAILED
IN THE
UNITED STATES

- - - - - - - - - - - - - Fold Here Second - - - - - - - - - - - - -